Anson D.F. Randolph

The Changed Cross, and Other Religious Poems

Anson D.F. Randolph

The Changed Cross, and Other Religious Poems

ISBN/EAN: 9783337256531

Printed in Europe, USA, Canada, Australia, Japan

Cover: Foto ©Thomas Meinert / pixelio.de

More available books at **www.hansebooks.com**

THE CHANGED CROSS

AND OTHER RELIGIOUS POEMS

COMPILED BY

ANSON D. F. RANDOLPH

NEW YORK
A. D. F. RANDOLPH CO.
1897

COPYRIGHT, 1872, BY
ANSON D. F. RANDOLPH & CO.

COPYRIGHT, 1897, BY
THE A. D. F. RANDOLPH CO.

THE CHANGED CROSS,

AND OTHER

RELIGIOUS POEMS.

IT was a time of sadness, and my heart,
Although it knew and loved the better part,
Felt wearied with the conflict and the strife,
And all the needful discipline of life.

And while I thought on these, as given to me—
My trial tests of faith and love to be—
It seemed as if I never could be sure
That faithful to the end I should endure.

And thus, no longer trusting to His might
Who says, "We walk by faith, and not by sight,"
Doubting, and almost yielding to despair,
The thought arose—My cross I can not bear.

Far heavier its weight must surely be
Than those of others which I daily see.
Oh! if I might another burden choose,
Methinks I should not fear my crown to lose.

A solemn silence reigned on all around—
E'en Nature's voices uttered not a sound;
The evening shadows seemed of peace to tell,
And sleep upon my weary spirit fell.

A moment's pause—and then a heavenly light
Beamed full upon my wondering, raptured sight
Angels on silvery wings seemed everywhere,
And angels' music thrilled the balmy air.

Then One, more fair than all the rest to see—
One to whom all the others bowed the knee—
Came gently to me as I trembling lay,
And, " Follow me ! " He said : " I am the Way."

Then, speaking thus, He led me far above,
And there, beneath a canopy of love,
Crosses of divers shape and size were seen,
Larger and smaller than my own had been.

And one there was, most beauteous to behold,
A little one, with jewels set in gold.
Ah! this, methought, I can with comfort wear,
For it will be an easy one to bear:

And so the little cross I quickly took;
But, all at once, my frame beneath it shook.
The sparkling jewels fair were they to *see*,
But far too heavy was their *weight* for me.

"This may not be," I cried, and looked again,
To see if there was any here could ease my pain
But, one by one, I passed them slowly by,
Till on a lovely one I cast my eye.

Fair flowers around its sculptured form entwined,
And grace and beauty seemed in it combined.
Wondering, I gazed; and still I wondered more
To think so many should have passed it o'er.

But oh! that form so beautiful to see
Soon made its hidden sorrows known to me;
Thorns lay beneath those flowers and colors fair!
Sorrowing, I said: "This cross I may not bear."

And so it was with each and all around—
Not one to suit my *need* could there be found;
Weeping, I laid each heavy burden down,
As my Guide gently said: "No cross, no crown!"

At length, to Him I raised my saddened heart:
He knew its sorrows, bid its doubts depart.
"Be not afraid," He said, "but trust in Me—
My perfect love shall now be shown to thee."

And then, with lightened eyes and willing feet,
Again I turned, my earthly cross to meet,
With forward footsteps, turning not aside,
For fear some hidden evil might betide;

And there—in the prepared, appointed w-
Listening to hear, and ready to obey—
A cross I quickly found of plainest form,
With only words of love inscribed thereon.

With thankfulness I raised it from the rest,
And joyfully acknowledged it the best—
The only one of all the many there
That I could feel was good for me to bear.

And, while I thus my chosen one confessed,
I saw a heavenly brightness on it rest;
And, as I bent, my burden to sustain,
I recognized my own old cross again.

But oh! how different did it seem to be,
Now I had learned its preciousness to see!
No longer could I unbelieving say,
Perhaps another is a better way.

Ah, no! henceforth my own desire shall be,
That He who knows me best should choose for me
And so, whate'er His love sees good to send,
I'll trust it's best, because He knows the end.

"For my thoughts are not your thoughts, saith the Lord."—
Isaiah 50: 8.

"For I know the thoughts that I think toward you—thoughts of peace, and not of evil, to give you an expected end."—Jer. 29: 11.

And when that happy time shall come, of endless peace and rest, We shall look back upon our path, and say: It was the best.

THE MEETING-PLACE.

WHERE the faded flower shall freshen,
   Freshen never more to fade;
Where the shaded sky shall brighten,
   Brighten never more to shade;
Where the sun-blaze never scorches;
   Where the star-beams cease to chill;
Where no tempest stirs the echoes
   Of the wood, or wave, or hill;
Where the morn shall wake in gladness,
   And the noon the joy prolong;
Where the daylight dies in fragrance
   'Mid the burst of holy song—
Brother, we shall meet and rest
'Mid the holy and the blest.

Where no shadow shall bewilder;
   Where life's vain parade is o'er;
Where the sleep of sin is broken,
   And the dreamer dreams no more;
Where the bond is never severed—
   Partings, claspings, sobs, and moan,
Midnight waking, twilight weeping,
   Heavy noontide—all are done;
Where the child has found its mother,
   Where the mother finds the child;

Where dear families are gathered
　　That were scattered on the wild—
Brother, we shall meet and rest
'Mid the holy and the blest.

Where the hidden wound is healed;
　　Where the blighted light re-blooms;
Where the smitten heart the freshness
　　Of its buoyant youth resumes;
Where the love that here we lavish
　　On the withering leaves of time,
Shall have fadeless flowers to fix on,
　　In an ever spring-bright clime;
Where we find the joy of loving,
　　As we never loved before;
Loving on unchilled, unhindered,
　　Loving once and evermore—
Brother, we shall meet and rest
'Mid the holy and the blest.

Where a blasted world shall brighten
　　Underneath a bluer sphere,
And a softer, gentler sunshine
　　Shed its healing splendor here;
Where earth's barren vales shall blossom,
　　Putting on their robe of green,
And a purer, fairer Eden
　　Be where only wastes have been;

Where a King, in kingly glory
   Such as earth has never known,
Shall assume the righteous scepter,
   Claim and wear the heavenly crown—
Brother, we shall meet and rest
'Mid the holy and the blest.

THE PILGRIM.

STILL onward through this land of foes
   I pass in Pilgrim guise;
I may not stop to seek repose;
   Where cool the shadow lies
I may not stoop amid the grass
   To pluck earth's fairest flowers,
Nor by her springing fountains pass
   The sultry noontide hours;

Yet flowers I wear upon my breast
   That no earth-garden knows—
White lilies of immortal peace,
   And love's deep-tinted rose;
And there the blue-eyed flowers of faith,
   And hope's bright buds of gold,
As lone I tread the upward path,
   In richest hues unfold.

I keep my armor ever on,
   For foes beset my way;
I watch, lest passing on alone,
   I fall a helpless prey.
No earthly love have I—I lean
   Upon no mortal breast;
But my Belovéd, though unseen,
   Walks near and gives me rest.

Afar, around, I often see,
   Throughout this desert wide,
His Pilgrims pressing on like me—
   They often pass my side:
The kindly smile, the gentle word,
   For Jesus' sake I give;
But love—O Thou alone adored!
   For Thee alone I live.

Painful and dark the pathway seems
   To distant earthly eyes;
They only see the hedging thorns
   On either side that rise;
They can not know how soft between
   The flowers of love are strewn—
The sunny ways, the pastures green,
   Where Jesus leads His own;

They can not see, as darkening clouds
   Behind the Pilgrim close,

How far adown the western glade
　The golden glory flows;
They can not hear 'mid earthly din
　The song to Pilgrims known,
Still blending with the angels' hymn
　Around the wondrous throne.

So I, Thy bounteous token-flowers
　Still on my bosom wear;
While me, the fleeting love-winged hours
　To Thee still nearer bear;
So from my lips Thy song shall flow,
　My sweetest music be;
So on mine eyes the glory grow,
　Till all is lost in Thee.

HOLY TEARS.

YES, thou may'st weep, for Jesus shed
　　Such tears as those thou sheddest now
When, for the living or the dead,
　Sorrow lay heavy on His brow.

He sees thee weep, yet doth not blame
　The weakness of thy flesh and heart;
Thy human nature is the same
　As that in which He took a part.

He knows its weakness, for He felt
    The crushing power of pain and woe;
How body, soul, and spirit melt,
    And faint beneath the stunning blow.

What if poor sinners count thy grief
    The sign of an unchastened will?
He who can give thy soul relief,
    Knows that thou art submissive still.

Turn thee to Him, to Him alone;
    For all that our poor lips can say
To soothe thee, broken-hearted one,
    Would fail to comfort thee to-day.

We will not speak to thee, but sit
    In prayerful silence by thy side:
Grief has its ebbs and flows; 'tis fit
    Our love should wait the ebbing tide.

Jesus Himself will comfort thee,
    In His own time, in His own way;
And haply more than "two or three"
    Unite in prayer for thee to-day.

GOD OUR STRENGTH.

MAN, in his weakness, needs a stronger stay
   Than fellow-men, the holiest and the best
And yet we turn to them from day to day,
   As if in them our spirits could find rest.

Gently untwine our childish hands, that cling
   To such inadequate supports as these,
And shelter us beneath Thy heavenly wing,
   Till we have learned to walk alone with ease.

Help us, O Lord! with patient love to bear
   Each other's faults, to suffer with true meekness;
Help us each other's joys and griefs to share,
   But let us turn to Thee alone in weakness.

WHOLLY RESIGNED.

CHRIST leads us through no darker rooms
   Than He went through before:
He that into God's kingdom comes,
   Must enter by this door:
Come, Lord, when grace hath made me meet
   Thy blessèd face to see,
For if Thy work on earth be sweet,
   What will Thy glory be!

Then I shall end my sad complaints,
  And weary, sinful days;
And join with the triumphant saints,
  That sing Jehovah's praise:
My knowledge of that life is small,
  The eye of faith is dim,
But 'tis enough that Christ knows all,
  And I shall be with Him.

"MY TIMES ARE IN THY HAND."

PSALM 31 : 15.

FATHER, I know that all my life
  Is portioned out for me;
And the changes that are sure to come,
  I do not fear to see;
But I ask Thee for a present mind
  Intent on pleasing Thee.

I ask Thee for a thankful love,
  Through constant watching wise,
To meet the glad with joyful smiles,
  And to wipe the weeping eyes,
And a heart at leisure from itself,
  To soothe and sympathize.

I would not have the restless will
  That hurries to and fro,
Seeking for some great thing to do,
  Or secret thing to know;
I would be dealt with as a child,
  And guided where to go.

Wherever in the world I am,
  In whatsoe'er estate,
I have a fellowship with hearts
  To keep and cultivate;
And a work of holy love to do
  For the Lord on whom I wait.

I ask Thee for the daily strength,
  To none that ask denied;
And a mind to blend with outward life
  While keeping at Thy side;
Content to fill a little space,
  If Thou be glorified.

And if some things I do not ask
  In my cup of blessing be,
I would have my spirit filled the more
  With grateful love to Thee—
More careful than to serve Thee much,
  To please Thee perfectly.

There are briers besetting every path,
  That call for patient care:

There is a crook in every lot,
   And a need for earnest prayer;
But a lonely heart that leans on Thee
   Is happy everywhere.

In a service that Thy love appoints
   There are no bonds for me,
For my secret heart is taught the truth
   That makes Thy children "free;"
And a life of self-renouncing love
   Is a life of liberty.

THE BORDER-LANDS.

FATHER, into Thy loving hands
   My feeble spirit I commit,
While wandering in these Border-Lands
   Until Thy voice shall summon it.

Father, I would not dare to choose
   A longer life, an earlier death;
I know not what my soul might lose
   By shortened or protracted breath.

These Border-Lands are calm and still,
   And solemn are their silent shades·
And my heart welcomes them, until
   The light of life's long evening fades.

I heard them spoken of with dread,
    As fearful and unquiet places;
Shades, where the living and the dead
    Look sadly in each other's faces.

But since Thy hand hath led me here,
    And I have seen the Border-Land,
Seen the dark river flowing near,
    Stood on its brink, as now I stand,

There has been nothing to alarm
    My trembling soul; how could I fear
While thus encircled with Thine arm?
    I never felt Thee half so near.

What should appal me in a place
    That brings me hourly nearer Thee?
When I may almost see Thy face—
    Surely 'tis here my soul would be.

They say the waves are dark and deep,
    That faith has perished in the river;
They speak of death with fear, and weep
    Shall my soul perish? Never! never

I know that Thou wilt never leave
    The soul that trembles while it clings
To Thee: I know Thou wilt achieve
    Its passage on Thine outspread wings

And since I first was brought so near
  The stream that flows to the Dead Sea,
I think that it has grown more clear
  And shallow than it used to be.

I can not see the golden gate
  Unfolding yet, to welcome me;
I can not yet anticipate
  The joy of heaven's jubilee;

But I will calmly watch and pray
  Until I hear my Saviour's voice
Calling my happy soul away,
  To see His glory and rejoice.

"ALL, ALL IS KNOWN TO THEE."

"When my spirit was overwhelmed within me, then Thou knewest my path."

MY God, whose gracious pity I may claim,
  Calling Thee Father—sweet, endearing name!
The sufferings of this weak and weary frame
  All, all are known to Thee.

From human eye 'tis better to conceal
Much that I suffer, much I hourly feel;
But oh! the thought does tranquillize and heal—
  All, all is known to Thee.

Each secret conflict with indwelling sin,
Each sickening fear I ne'er the prize shall win,
Each pang from irritation, turmoil, din—
    All, all are known to Thee.

When in the morning unrefreshed I wake,
Or in the night but little sleep can take,
This brief appeal submissively I make—
    All, all is known to Thee.

Nay, all by Thee is ordered, chosen, planned—
Each drop that fills my daily cup; Thy hand
Prescribes for ills none else can understand.
    All, all is known to Thee.

The effectual means to cure what I deplore,
In me Thy longed-for likeness to restore;
Self to dethrone, never to govern more—
    All, all are known to Thee.

And this continued feebleness, this state
Which seems to unnerve and incapacitate,
Will work the cure my hopes and prayers await—
    That can I leave to Thee.

Nor will the bitter draught distasteful prove,
When I recall the SON of Thy dear love;
The cup Thou wouldst not for *our* sakes remove
    That cup He drank for *me*.

He drank it to the dregs—no drop remained
Of wrath, for those whose cup of woe He drained
Man ne'er can know what that sad cup contained.
    All, all is known to Thee.

And welcome, *precious*, can His Spirit make
My little drop of suffering for His sake.
Father, the cup I drink, the path I take,
    All, all is known to Thee.

OH! FOR THE HAPPY DAYS GONE BY.

OH! for the happy days gone by,
    When love ran smooth and free;
Days when my spirit so enjoyed
    More than earth's liberty!

Oh! for the times when on my heart
    Long prayer had never palled;
Times when the ready thought of God
    Would come when it was called!

Then when I knelt to meditate,
    Sweet thoughts came oe'r my soul,
Countless, and bright, and beautiful,
    Beyond my own control.

Oh! who hath locked those fountains up?
    Those visions who hath staid?

What sudden act hath thus transformed
  My sunshine into shade?

This freezing heart, O Lord! this will,
  Dry as the desert sand—
Good thoughts that will not come, bad thoughts
  That come without command—

A faith that seems not faith, a hope
  That cares not for its aim—
A love that none the hotter grows
  At Jesus' blessèd name—

The weariness of prayer, the mist
  O'er conscience overspread—
The chill repugnance to frequent
  The feast of angels' bread:

If this drear change be Thine, O Lord!
  If it be Thy sweet will,
Spare not, but to the very brim
  The bitter chalice fill;

But if it hath been sin of mine,
  Oh! show that sin to me—
Not to get back the sweetness lost,
  But to make peace with Thee.

One thing alone, dear Lord, I dread—
  To have a secret spot

That separates my soul from Thee,
　And yet to know it not.

Oh! when the tide of graces set
　So full upon my heart,
I know, dear Lord, how faithlessly
　I did my little part.

I know how well my heart hath earned
　A chastisement like this,
In trifling many a grace away
　In self-complacent bliss.

But if this weariness hath come
　A present from on high,
Teach me to find the hidden wealth
　That in its depths may lie;

So in this darkness I can learn
　To tremble and adore,
To sound my own vile nothingness,
　And thus to love Thee more;

To love Thee, and yet not to think
　That I can love so much;
To have Thee with me, Lord! all day
　Yet not to feel Thy touch.

If I have served Thee, Lord! for hire,
　Hire which Thy beauty showed.

Ah! I can serve Thee now for naught,
And only as my God.

Oh! blessed be this darkness, then,
This deep in which I lie;
And blessed be all things that teach
God's dread supremacy!

LOST TREASURES.

LET us be patient—God has taken from us
The earthly treasures upon which we leaned,
That from the fleeting things which lie around us,
Our clinging hearts should be forever weaned.

They have passed from us—all our broad possessions:
Ships, whose white sails flung wide past distant shores;
Lands, whose rich harvests smiled in the glad sunshine;
Silver and gold, and all our hoarded stores.

And, dearer far, the pleasant home where gathered
Our loved and loving round the blazing hearth,
Where honored age on the soft cushions rested,
And childhood played about in frolic mirth

Where underneath the softened light bent kindly
  The mother's tender glance on daughters fair,
And he on whom all leant with fond confiding,
  Rested contented from his daily care.

All shipwrecked in one common desolation!
  The garden-walks by other feet are trod;
The clinging vines by other fingers tutored
  To fling their shadows o'er the grassy sod.

While carking care and deep humiliation
  In tears are mingled with their daily bread;
And the rude blasts we never thought could reach us,
  Have spent their worst on each defenseless head.

Let us be cheerful! The same sky o'erarches—
  Soft rain falls on the evil and the good;
On narrow walls, and through our humbler dwelling,
  God's glorious sunshine pours as rich a flood.

Faith, hope, and love still in our hearts abiding,
  May bear their precious fruits in us the same,
And to the couch of suffering we may carry,
  If but the cup of water, in His name.

Let us be thankful, if in this affliction
  No grave is opened for the loving heart;
And while we bend beneath our Father's chiding
  We yet can mourn "each family apart."

Shoulder to shoulder let us breast the torrent,
　With not one cold reproach nor angry look ;
There are some seasons, when the heart is smitten,
　It can no whisper of unkindness brook.

Our life is not in all these brief possessions ;
　Our home is not in any pleasant spot :
Pilgrims and strangers, we must journey onward,
　Contented with the portion of our lot.

These earthly walls must shortly be dismantled ;
　These earthly tents be struck by angel hands ;
But to be built up on a sure foundation,
　　There, where our Father's mansion ever stands.

There shall we meet, parent and child, and dearer
　That earthly love which makes half heaven of
　　home ;
There shall we find our treasures all awaiting,
　Where change and death and parting nevei
　　come.

SUNDAY.

"I was in the spirit on the Lord's day."—REV. 1 : 10.

AFTER long days of storms and showers,
　Of sighing winds, and dripping bowers
How sweet, at morn, to ope our eyes
On newly "swept and garnished" skies !

To miss the clouds, and driving rain,
And see that all is bright again—
So bright we can not choose but say,
Is this the world of yesterday?

Even so, methinks, the Sunday brings
A change o'er all familiar things;
A change—we know not whence it came—
They are, and they are not, the same.

There is a spell within, around,
On eye and ear, on sight and sound;
And, loth or willing, they and we
Must own this day a mystery.

Sure all things wear a heavenly dress
That sanctifies their loveliness,—
Types of that endless resting-day,
When "we shall all be changed" as they.

To-day our peaceful, ordered home
Foreshadoweth mansions yet to come;
We foretaste, in domestic love,
The faultless charities above.

And as at yester-eventide
Our tasks and toys were laid aside,
Lo! here our training for the day
When we shall lay them down for aye.

But not alone for musings deep,
Meek souls their "day of days" will keep
Yet other glorious things than these
The Christian in his Sabbath sees.

His eyes, by faith, his Lord behold;
How on the week's first day of old
From hell he rose, on Death he trod,
Was seen of men, and went to God.

And as we fondly pause to look
Where in some daily-handled book,
Approval's well-known tokens stand,
Traced by some dear and thoughtful hand

Even so there shines one day in seven
Bright with the special mark of Heaven,
That we with love and praise may dwell
On Him who loveth us so well.

Whether in meditative walk,
Alone with God and heaven we talk,
Catching the simple chime that calls
Our feet to some old church's walls;

Or passed within the church's door,
Where poor are rich, and rich are poor,
We say the prayers, and hear the word,
Which there our fathers said and heard;

Or represent in solemn wise
Our all-prevailing sacrifice;
Feeding in joint communion high,
The life of faith that can not die.

And surely, in a world like this,
So rife with woe, so scant of bliss—
Where fondest hopes are oftenest crossed
And fondest hopes are severed most;

'Tis something that we kneel and pray
With loved ones near and far away;
One God, one faith, one hope, one care,
One form of words, one hour of prayer.

'Tis just—yet pause, till ear and heart,
In one brief silence, ere we part,
Somewhat of that high strain have caught,
" The peace of God which passeth thought."

Then turn we to our earthly homes,
Not doubting but that Jesus comes,
Breathing His peace on hall and hut
At evening, when the doors are shut.

Then speeds us on our work-day way,
And hallows every common day;
Without *Him* Sunday's self were dim,
But all are bright, *if spent with Him*.

ONE BY ONE.

ONE by one the sands are flowing,
   One by one the moments fall;
Some are coming, some are going—
   Do not strive to grasp them all.

One by one thy duties wait thee.
   Let thy whole strength go to each:
Let no future dreams elate thee:
   Learn thou first what those can teach

One by one (bright gifts from heaven)
   Joys are sent thee here below:
Take them readily, when given—
   Ready, too, to let them go.

One by one thy griefs shall meet thee
   Do not fear an armèd band;
One will fade, while others greet thee
   Shadows passing through the land.

Do not look at life's long sorrow,
   See how small each moment's pain
God will help thee for to-morrow—
   Every day begin again.

Every hour that fleets so slowly,
   Has its task to do or bear;

Luminous the crown, and holy,
  If thou set each gem with care.

Do not linger with regretting,
  Or for passion's hour despond,
Nor, the daily toil forgetting,
  Look too eagerly beyond.

Hours are golden links, God's token
  Reaching heaven, but one by one
Take them, lest the chain be broken
  Ere the pilgrimage be done.

MARY'S CHOICE.

JESUS, engrave it on my heart,
  That Thou the one thing needful art
I could from all things parted be,
But never, never, Lord, from Thee.

Needful is Thy most precious blood,
Needful is Thy correcting rod;
Needful is Thy indulgent care,
Needful Thy all-prevailing prayer.

Needful Thy presence, dearest Lord,
True peace and comfort to afford;

Needful Thy promise to impart
Fresh life and vigor to my heart.

Needful art Thou to be my stay
Through all life's dark and thorny way;
Nor less in death Thou'lt needful be,
To bring my spirit home to Thee.

Then needful still, my God, my King,
Thy name eternally I'll sing;
Glory and praise be ever His—
The "one thing needful" Jesus is.

"*NEARER HOME.*" *

ONE sweetly solemn thought
   Comes to me o'er and o'er;
I am nearer home to-day
   Than I ever have been before:

Nearer my Father's house,
   Where the many mansions be;
Nearer the great white throne,
   Nearer the crystal sea:

Nearer the bound of life,
   Where we lay our burdens down;

---

* As this poem has suffered many changes in the various reprints, the author, in the year 1867, furnished the present publishers with this correct copy.

Nearer leaving the cross,
  Nearer gaining the crown.

But lying darkly between,
  Winding down through the night,
Is the silent, unknown stream,
  That leads at last to the light

Closer and closer my steps
  Come to the dark abysm;
Closer death to my lips
  Presses the awful chrysm.

Oh, if my mortal feet
  Have almost gained the brink;
If it be I am nearer home,
  Even to-day than I think;

Father, perfect my trust,
  Let my spirit feel in death,
That her feet are firmly set
  On the rock of a living faith!

OH! TO BE READY.

OH! to be ready when death shall come
  Oh! to be ready to hasten home!
No earthward clinging, no lingering gaze,
No strife at parting, no sore amaze·

No chains to sever that earth hath twined,
No spell to loosen that love would bind.

No flitting shadows to dim the light
Of the angel-pinions winged for flight;
No cloud-like phantoms to fling a gloom
'Twixt heaven's bright portals and earth's dark
    tomb;
But sweetly, gently, to pass away
From the world's dim twilight into day.

To list the music of angel lyres,
To catch the rapture of seraph fires,
To lean in trust on the risen One,
Till borne away to a fadeless throne.
Oh! to be ready when death shall come!
Oh! to be ready to hasten home!

THE BRIDEGROOM'S DOVE.

*"O my Dove! in the clefts of the rock, in the secret of the stairs."—*Cant. 2: 14.

"MY DOVE!" The Bridegroom speaks. To
whom?
  Whom, think'st thou, meaneth He?
Say, O my soul! canst thou presume
  He thus addresseth thee?

Yes, 'tis the Bridegroom's voice of love,
Calling thee, O my soul, His Dove!

The Dove is gentle, mild, and meek:
  Deserve I, then, the name?
I look within in vain to seek
  Aught which can give a claim·
Yet, made so by redeeming love,
My soul, thou art the Bridegroom's Dove!

Methinks, my soul, that thou may'st see,
  In this endearing word,
Reasons why Jesus likens thee
  To this defenseless bird;
Reasons which show the Bridegroom's love
To His poor, helpless, timid Dove!

The Dove, of all the feathered tribe,
  Doth least of power possess
My soul: what better can describe
  Thine utter helplessness?
Yet courage take! the Bridegroom's love
Will keep, defend, protect His Dove!

The Dove hath neither claw nor sting,
  Nor weapon for the fight;
She owes her safety to her wing,
  Her victory to flight.

A shelter hath the Bridegroom's love
Provided for His helpless Dove.

The Hawk comes on, in eager chase—
  The Dove will not resist;
In flying to her hiding-place,
  Her safety doth consist.
The Bridegroom opes His arms of love,
And in them folds His panting Dove!

Nothing the Dove can now molest,
  Safe from the fowler's snare;
The Bridegroom's bosom is her nest—
  Nothing can harm her there.
Encircled by the arms of love,
Almighty power protects the Dove!

As the poor Dove, before the Hawk
  Quick to her refuge flies,
So need I, in my daily walk,
  The wing which faith supplies,
To bear me where the Bridegroom's love
Places beyond all harm His Dove!

My soul, of native power bereft,
  To Calvary repairs;

Immanuel is the *rocky cleft*,
  "*The secret of the stairs!*"
Since placed *there* by the Bridegroom's love
What evil can befall His Dove?

Though Sinai's thunder round her roars,
  Though Ebal's lightnings flash,
Though heaven a fiery torrent pours,
  And riven mountains crash—
Through all, the "still small voice" of love
Whispers: "Be not afraid, my Dove!"

What though the heavens away may pass,
  With fervent heat dissolve,
And round the sun this earthly mass
  No longer shall revolve?
Behold a miracle of love!
The lion quakes, but not the Dove!

My soul, now hid within a rock
  (The "Rock of Ages" called),
Amid the universal shock
  Is fearless, unappalled:
A cleft therein, prepared by love,
In safety hides the Bridegroom's Dove!

O happy Dove! thus weak, thus safe;
  Do I resemble her?

Then to my soul, O Lord! vouchsafe
A *dove-like* character!
Pure, harmless, gentle, full of love,
Make me in spirit, Lord, a Dove!

O Thou, who on the Bridegroom's head
   Didst, as a Dove, come down,
Within my soul Thy graces shed,
   Establish there Thy throne;
There shed abroad a Saviour's love,
Thou holy, pure, and heavenly Dove!

GOD, MY EXCEEDING JOY.

PSALM 43 : 4.

EARLY my spirit turned
   From earthly things away,
And agonized and yearned
   For the eternal day;
Dimly I saw, when but a boy,
   God, my exceeding joy.

In days of fiercer flame,
   When passion urged me on,
Twas only bliss in name—
   The pleasure soon was gone.

Compared with Thee, how all things cloy,
  God, my exceeding joy!

At length the moment came—
  Jesus made known His love;
High shot the kindling flame
  To glories all above.
Now all my powers one theme employ:
  God, my exceeding joy.

Shadows came on apace;
  Tears were a pensive shower;
I cried for timely grace
  To save me from the hour;
Thou gavest peace without alloy,
  God, my exceeding joy.

One trial yet awaits,
  Gigantic at the close;
All that my spirit hates
  May then my peace oppose;
But God shall this last foe destroy
  God, my exceeding joy.

GOD'S SUPPORT AND GUIDANCE.

TRANSLATED FROM THE GERMAN.

FORSAKE me not, my God,
Thou God of my salvation!
Give me Thy light, to be
My sure illumination.
My soul to folly turns,
Seeking she knows not what;
Oh! lead her to Thyself—
My God, forsake me not!

Forsake me not, my God!
Take not Thy Spirit from me,
And suffer not the might
Of sin to overcome me.
A father pitieth
The children he begot;
My Father, pity me—
My God, forsake me not.

Forsake me not, my God;
Thou God of life and power,
Enliven, strengthen me
In every evil hour;
And when the sinful fire
Within my heart is hot,

Be not Thou far from me—
  My God, forsake me not!

Forsake me not, my God!
  Uphold me in my going,
That evermore I may
  Please Thee in all well-doing,
And that Thy will, O Lord!
  May never be forgot,
In all my works and ways—
  My God, forsake me not!

Forsake me not, my God!
  I would be thine forever!
Confirm me mightily
  In every right endeavor;
And when my hour is come,
  Cleansed from all stain and spot
Of sin, receive my soul—
  My God, forsake me not!

I AM.

"God calls himself I AM, leaving a blank which each soul may fill up with that which is most precious to himself."

THOU bidd'st us call, and giv'st us many a name,
That Thou may'st hear and answer every cry,
But—for the wants of all are not the same—
Another name Thy wondrous love did try;
To Moses first Thou gav'st it, and he knew
Its worth, and taught us how to prize it, too :
I AM—let every sinner kneel, and thank
The Lord, and with his wants fill up the blank.
Thy very wounds do say, each drop they bleed,
"I AM thy need."

Oh! I am weary of this life,
  Of all its vanity and care;
Where can I hide me from its strife,
  From all its noises—where?
My spirit sinks beneath the load,
I pant to reach a safe abode.
When shall I find a sweet release?
Remains there yet a lasting peace,
A calm for my long storm-tost breast?
  "I AM thy rest."

Oh! I am full of grievous sin,
    I can do naught that's right;
O God! how base my soul is in
    Thy pure and holy sight!
Thy perfect laws I daily, hourly break,
And will not yield my will for Thy sweet sake,
Still in my soul do burn wicked desires,
And my heart's altar bears unhallowed fires;
I can do naught but all these things confess,
      "I AM thy righteousness."

But, Lord, I am so weak, so weak,
    I can not stand before Thy face;
Thy praises I can hardly speak,
    Hardly stretch forth my hands for grace;
The way seems long—the burden who can bear?
Lord, must I sink beneath the load of care?
Thus is it now; what shall it be at length?
      "I AM thy strength."

Lord, I must die; e'en now the wing
    Of Thy dread angel hovereth nigh;
I know the message he doth bring—
    "Soul, thou hast sinned, and thou must die."
All nature feels and owns the just decree;
And is this all that is in store for me—
Ashes to ashes, dust to kindred dust,
No hope, no light? Surely my spirit must

Sink in despair ere nature's last, fierce strife—
"I AM thy life."

Oh, wonderful Thou art!
Too wonderful for me is such great love,
Shining in such a heart
   Like sunbeams from above.
How rich am I! yea, all things I possess—
Peace, joy, life, strength, and perfect righteous-
   ness.
Jehovah shows Himself, and gives to me
All my desire. Look, trembling soul! and see
On what a treasury thy want may call—
   "I AM thine all in all."

A LITTLE WHILE.

BEYOND the smiling and the weeping
   I shall be soon;
Beyond the waking and the sleeping,
Beyond the sowing and the reaping,
   I shall be soon.
   Love, rest, and home!
     Sweet hope!
   Lord, tarry not, but come.

Beyond the blooming and the fading
  I shall be soon:
Beyond the shining and the shading,
Beyond the hoping and the dreading,
  I shall be soon.
    Love, rest, and home!
      Sweet hope!
    Lord, tarry not, but come.

Beyond the rising and the setting
  I shall be soon;
Beyond the calming and the fretting,
Beyond remembering and forgetting,
  I shall be soon.
    Love, rest, and home!
      Sweet hope!
    Lord, tarry not, but come.

Beyond the gathering and the strewing
  I shall be soon;
Beyond the ebbing and the flowing,
Beyond the coming and the going,
  I shall be soon.
    Love, rest, and home!
      Sweet hope!
    Lord, tarry not, but come.

Beyond the parting and the meeting
  I shall be soon;

Beyond the farewell and the greeting,
Beyond this pulse's fever-beating,
  I shall be soon.
    Love, rest, and home!
      Sweet hope!
  Lord, tarry not, but come.

Beyond the frost-chain and the fever
  I shall be soon;
Beyond the rock-waste and the river;
Beyond the ever and the never,
  I shall be soon.
    Love, rest, and home!
      Sweet hope!
  Lord, tarry not, but come.

HINDER ME NOT.

HINDER me not! the path is long and weary,
  I may not pause nor tarry by the way;
Night cometh, when no man may journey onward,
  For we must walk as children of the day.

I know the city lieth fair behind me,
  The very brightest gem that studs the plain;
But thick and fast the lurid clouds are rising
  Which soon shall scatter into fiery rain.

I must press on until I reach my Zoar,
  And there find refuge from the fearful blast.
In Thy cleft side, O smitten Saviour! hide me,
  Till the calamity be overpast.

Ye can not tempt me back with pomp or pleasure,
  All, in my eager grasp, have turned to dust:
The shield of love around my hearth is broken;
  How shall I place on man's frail life my trust?

But my heart lingers when I pass the dwellings
  Where children play about the open door;
And pleasant voices waken up the echoes,
  From silent lips of those I see no more.

For through their chambers swept the solemn warning,
  Arise! depart! for this is not your rest;
They folded their pale hands and sought the presence—
  I only bore the arrow in my breast.

But there is balm in Gilead, and a Healer
  Whose sovereign power can cure our every ill.
And to the soul, more wildly tempest-tossing
  Than ever Galilee, say: "Peace, be still!"

Who, showing His own name thereon engraven,
  With bleeding hands will draw the dart again.

And whisper : "Should the true disciple murmur
To taste the cup his Master's lip could drain ? "

And then lead on until we reach the river
  Which all must cross, and some must cross
    alone:
Oh! ye who in the land of peace are wearied,
  How shall ye breast the Jordan's swelling moan ?

I know not if the wave shall rage or slumber,
  When I shall stand upon the nearer shore ;
But one whose form the Son of God resembleth,
  Will cross with me, and I shall ask no more.

O weary heads ! rest on your Saviour's bosom ;
  O weary feet ! press on the path He trod ;
O weary souls ! your rest shall be remaining,
  When ye have gained the city of your God.

O glorious city ! jasper built, and shining
  With God's own glory in effulgent light,
Wherein no manner of defilement cometh,
  Nor any shadow flung from passing night.

There shall ye pluck fruits from that tree immortal,
  And be like gods, but find no curse therein :
There shall ye slake your thirst in that full fount-
    ain   [sin.
Whose distant streams sufficed to cleanse your

There shall ye find your dead in Christ arisen,
    And learn from them to sing the angels' song
Well may ye echo from earth's waiting prison,
    The martyr's cry: "How long, O Lord! how
        long!"

"I CLING TO THEE."

O HOLY Saviour, Friend unseen!
    Since on Thine arm Thou bidst me lean,
Help me throughout life's varying scene—
    By faith I cling to Thee.

Blest with this fellowship divine,
Take what Thou wilt, I'll ne'er repine;
E'en as the branches to the vine,
    My soul would cling to Thee.

Far from her home, fatigued, oppressed,
Here has she found her place of rest.
An exile still, yet not unblessed,
    While she can cling to Thee.

What though the world deceitful prove
And earthly friends and joys remove,
With patient uncomplaining love,
    Still would I cling to Thee.

Though faith and hope may long be tried,
I ask not, need not aught beside ;
How safe, how calm, how satisfied,
    The soul that clings to Thee !

They fear not Satan, nor the grave ;
They feel Thee near, and strong to save ;
Nor dread to cross e'en Jordan's wave,
    Because they cling to Thee !

Blest is my lot—whate'er befall ;
What can disturb me—who appal ?
While, as my strength, my rock, my all,
    Saviour, I cling to Thee !

"ALONE, YET NOT ALONE."

WHEN no kind earthly friend is near,
    With gentle words my heart to cheer,
Still am I with my Saviour dear :
    "Alone, yet not alone."

Though no loved forms my path attend,
With tender looks o'er me to bend,
Yet I am with my unseen Friend :
    "Alone, yet not alone."

When sorely racked with pain and grief,
Here I can find a sure relief ;

And I rejoice in the belief:
    "Alone, yet not alone."

'Tis on His strength that I rely,
And doubts and fears at once defy,
So happy, so content am I,
    "Alone, yet not alone."

E'en when with friends my lot is cast,
And words of love are flowing fast,
Still am I, when those hours are past,
    "Alone, yet not alone."

If all my earthly friends remove,
My fondest wishes empty prove,
Still am I with my Saviour's love
    "Alone, yet not alone."

Whate'er may now to me betide,
I have a place wherein to hide
By faith: 'tis e'en at His blest side:
    "Alone, yet not alone."

THE SCHOOL OF SUFFERING.

SAVIOUR, beneath Thy yoke
    My wayward heart doth pine;
All unaccustomed to the stroke
  Of love divine:

Thy chastisements, my God, are hard to bear,
Thy cross is heavy for frail flesh to wear.

"Perishing child of clay!
    Thy sighing I have heard;
Long have I marked thy evil way,
    How thou hast erred!
Yet fear not, by my own most holy name
I will shed healing through thy sin-sick frame.

"Praise to Thee, gracious Lord!
    I fain would be at rest;
Oh! now fulfill Thy faithful word,
    And make me blest;
My soul would lay her heavy burden down,
And take, with joyfulness, the promised crown.

"Stay, thou short-sighted child!
    There is much first to do—
Thy heart, so long by sin defiled,
    I must renew;
Thy will must here be taught to bend to mine,
Or the sweet peace of heaven can ne'er be thine

"Yea, Lord, but Thou canst soon
    Perfect Thy work in me,
Till, like the pure, calm summer noon,
    I shine by Thee;

A moment shine, that all Thy power may trace
Then pass in stillness to my heavenly place.

"Ah! coward soul, confess
    Thou shrinkest from my cure,
Thou tremblest at the sharp distress
    Thou must endure,
The foes on every hand for war arrayed,
The thorny path in tribulation laid;

"The process slow of years,
    The discipline of life;
Of outward woes and secret tears,
    Sickness and strife;
Thine idols taken from thee, one by one,
Till thou canst dare to live with me alone.

"Some gentle souls there are,
    Who yield unto my love,
Who, ripening fast beneath my care,
    I soon remove;
But thou stiff-necked art, and hard to rule;
Thou must stay longer in affliction's school."

My Maker and my King!
    Is this Thy love to me?
Oh! that I had the lightning's wing,
    From earth to flee:

How can I bear the heavy weight of woes
Thine indignation on the creature throws?

"Thou canst not, O my child!
  So hear my voice again;
I will bear all thy anguish wild,
  Thy grief, thy pain;
My arms shall be around thee, day by day,
My smile shall cheer thee on thy heavenward way

"In sickness, I will be
  Watching beside thy bed;
In sorrow thou shalt lean on me
  Thy aching head;
In every struggle thou shalt conqueror prove,
Nor death itself shall sever from my love."

O grace beyond compare!
  O love most high and pure!
Saviour, begin, no longer spare,
  I can endure;
Only vouchsafe Thy grace, that I may live
Unto Thy glory, who canst so forgive.

THE PILGRIM'S WANTS.

I WANT that adorning divine,
  Thou, only, my God, canst bestow;
I want in those beautiful garments to shine,
  Which distinguish Thy household below.
                      Col. 3 : 12-17.

I want, oh! I want to attain
  Some likeness, my Saviour, to Thee:
That longed-for resemblance once more to regain
  Thy comeliness put upon me.
                      1 John 3 : 2, 3.

I want to be marked for Thy own;
  Thy seal on my forehead to wear;
To receive that "new name" on the mystic white
    stone,
Which only Thyself canst declare.
                      Rev. 2 : 17.

I want, every moment, to feel
  That the Spirit does dwell in my heart;
That His power is present to cleanse and to heal
  And newness of life to impart.
                      Rom. 8 · 11-16.

I want so in Thee to abide,
  As to bring forth some fruit to Thy praise,

The branch that Thou prunest, though feeble and
   dried,
May languish, but never decays.
                              John 15 : 2-5.

I want Thine own hand to unbind
  Each tie to terrestrial things,
Too tenderly cherished, too closely entwined,
  Where my heart too tenaciously clings.
                              1 John 2 : 15.

I want, by my aspect serene,
  My actions and words, to declare
That my treasure is placed in a country unseen,
  That my heart and affections are there.
                              Matt. 6 : 19-21.

I want, as a traveler, to haste
  Straight onward, nor pause on my way;
No forethought or anxious contrivance to waste
  On my tent, only pitched for a day.
                              Heb. 13 · 5. 6

I want (and this sums up my prayer)
  To glorify Thee till I die;
Then calmly to yield up my soul to Thy care,
  And breathe out in prayer my last sigh.
                              Phil. 3 : 8, 9

HEAVEN.

OH! heaven is nearer than mortals think,
    When they look with a trembling dread
At the misty future that stretches on,
    From the silent home of the dead.

'Tis no lone isle on a boundless main,
    No brilliant but distant shore,
Where the lovely ones who are called away
    Must go to return no more.

No, heaven is near us; the mighty veil
    Of mortality blinds the eye,
That we can not see the angel bands,
    On the shores of eternity.

The eye that shuts in a dying hour,
    Will open the next in bliss;
The welcome will sound in the heavenly world
    Ere the farewell is hushed in this.

We pass from the clasp of mourning friends,
    To the arms of the loved and lost,
And those smiling faces will greet us there
    Which on earth we have valued most.

Yet oft in the hours of holy thought,
    To the thirsting soul is given

That power to pierce through the mist of sense,
To the beauteous scenes of heaven.

Then very near seem its pearly gates,
　And sweetly its harpings fall;
Till the soul is restless to soar away,
　And longs for the angel's call.

I know when the silver cord is loosed,
　When the veil is rent away,
Not long and dark shall the passage be,
　To the realms of endless day.

A VOICE FROM HEAVEN.

I SHINE in the light of God,
　His image stamps my brow;
Through the shadows of Death my feet have trod,
　And I reign in glory now.
No breaking heart is here,
　No keen and thrilling pain;
No wasted cheek, where the burning tear
　Hath rolled, and left its stain.

I have found the joys of heaven,
　I am one of the angel band;
To my head a crown is given,
　And a harp is in my hand;

I have learned the song they sing,
　Whom Jesus hath made free,
And tne glorious walls of heaven still ring
　With my new-born melody.

No sin, no grief, no pain—
　Safe in my happy home;
My fears all fled, my doubts all slain,
　My hour of triumph come.
Oh, friends of my mortal years!
　The trusted and the true,
You're walking still the vale of tears,
　But I wait to welcome you.

Do I forget? Oh! no,
　For memory's golden chain
Shall bind my heart to the hearts below
　Till they meet and touch again;
Each link is strong and bright,
　While love's electric flame
Flows freely down, like a river of light
　To the world from whence I came.

Do you mourn when another star
　Shines out from the glorious sky?
Do you weep when the voice of war
　And the rage of conflict die?

Why then should your tears roll down,
Or your heart be sorely riven,
For another gem in the Saviour's crown,
And another soul in heaven?

SUPPLICATION.

LORD, hear my prayer!
Turn not Thine ear from my distress,
But with Thy loving mercy bless,
Lest I despair.

Be gracious, Lord!
My soul is oft opprest and weak;
Oh! aid when I comfort seek
In Thy blest word.

My footsteps stray;
I wander oft from the road
That leads to peace and Thee, my God.
Teach Thou the way.

Oh! make me pure,
Clothe Thou my soul in spotless white,
That my acceptance in Thy sight
Be always sure.

Let me be one
Of all the sinless company

That round Thy throne hosannas sing
Through Christ Thy Son.

Thy will be done
On earth, as by each holy one,
Thy own redeemed, who near Thy throne
Bow down the knee!

EVENING PRAYER.

FATHER of mercy! at the close of day,
  My work and duties done, to Thee I pray
    Before I sleep;
With claspèd hands I humbly bow my head
And ask Thee, Lord, ere I retire to bed,
    My soul to keep.

The sins and failings of the day now past,
The shadows on my soul that they have cast
    Do Thou forgive;
Oh! purge my life from every taint of sin,
That I within Thy courts may enter in,
    With Thee to live.

Whatever sorrow I this day have known,
I spread it now, O Lord! before Thy throne—
    Oh! succor send;
I would beneath Thy chastening hand be still

And meekly bow before Thy sovereign will,
    Unto the end.

And now, with folded hand upon my breast,
At peace with Thee, I lay me down to rest
    Upon my bed ;
May angels guard me through the darksome night
From troubled dreams, until the morning light
    Its beams shall shed.

THE WANDERING HEART.

ALAS ! for the wildly wandering heart,
    And its changing idol guests !
It has roamed away to the world's far ends,
  At the vagrant wind's behests.
More fleet in its course than the flying dart—
  Alas ! for the wandering heart.

Go, bind it with Memory's holiest spells,
  But it recks not the things of old ;
Go, chain it in Gratitude's surest cells,
  With fetters more precious than gold·
Yet ever, oh ! ever, it will depart—
  Alas ! for the wandering heart.

Is it gone up to listen at heaven's gate,
  To Gabriel's lyre of praise?
And to catch the deep chanting where seraphs wait
  As a lesson for its mortal lays?
Oh, no! for it loves from such lessons to part—
  Alas! for the wandering heart.

It loves on a worthless and treacherous world
  To bestow its high desires;
And the lamp which it ought to be lighting in heaven,
  It kindles at idol fires.
Full seldom it turns to its guiding chart—
  Alas! for the wandering heart.

It needs to be steeped in the briny wave
  Of affliction's billowy sea,
And salt tears must water its way to the grave,
  Ere it will from these vanities flee.
It must ever be feeling the chastening smart—
  Alas! for the wandering heart.

My Father! my Father! this heart would be Thine,
  Restore from its wanderings;
Oh! visit and nourish thy wilderness vine,
  Though it be from the bitter springs:
Till the years of its pruning in time shall be o'er
And its shoots in eternity wander no more!

"RETURN THEE TO THY REST."

RETURN, return thee to thine only rest,
Lone pilgrim of the world!
Far erring from the fold—
By the dark night and risen storms distressed :
List, weary lamb, the Shepherd's anxious voice
And once again within His arms rejoice.

Return, return, thy fair white fleece is soiled,
   And by sharp briers rent—
   Thy little strength is spent ;
Yet He will pity thee, thou torn and spoiled.
There, thou art cradled on His tender breast ;
Now never more, sweet lamb, forsake that rest.

Return, return, my soul ; be like this lamb ;
   Yet can it, can it be
   That thou should'st pardon me,
Thou injured love! all ingrate as I am ;
Once again, weary of earth's trifling things,
False as the desert's far and shining springs?

Return, return to thy forsaken Friend,
   So long despised, forgot—
That now, thou wandering heart, 'twere just
   If He should "know thee not ; "

Yet on, press on, toward the mercy-seat,
And if thou perish, perish at His feet.

Return, return, for He is near thee dwelling,
   And not into the air
   Need rise the sighs of prayer;
Into His ear thou'rt all thy sorrows telling,
Thou need'st not speak to Him through spaces
For He is near thee, even at thy side.   [wide,

"Him have I pierced"—oh! I come, I come;
   My heart is broken, Lord,
   It needs nor voice nor word;
One only look brought Peter back of yore;
How bitterly I weep as then he wept!
Henceforth, oh! keep me, and I shall be kept.

NEAR JESUS.

I WANT to live near Jesus,
   And never go astray,
To feel that I am growing
   More like Him every day;
That I am always laying
   My treasure up above,
And gaining more the spirit
   Of His gentleness and love.

I want such steadfast purpose
  My mission to fulfill,
That it may be my meat and drink
  To do my Father's will;
To follow in His footsteps,
  Who never turned aside
From the path that leads to heaven
  Though often sorely tried.

Oh! that in His humility
  My spirit may be clad!
That I may have the patience
  My suffering Saviour had;
A heart more disengagèd
  From earth and earthly things,
Which through life's varied trials
  To Jesus simply clings.

Oh! I shall live near Jesus,
  And never go astray,
And every sin-defiling stain
  Shall soon be washed away;
And I'll bear my Master's image
  When I see Him face to face;
Then earth shall lose the power
  Its brightness to deface.

WHO IS MY BROTHER?

MUST I my brother keep,
  And share his pains and toils,
And weep with those that weep,
  And smile with those that smile;
And act to each a brother's part,
And feel his sorrows in my heart?

Must I his burden bear
  As though it were my own,
And do as I would care
  Should to myself be done;
And faithful to his interests prove,
And as myself my neighbor love?

Must I reprove his sin,
  Must I partake his grief,
And kindly enter in
  And minister relief—
The naked clothe, the hungry feed,
And love him, not in word, but deed?

Then, Jesus, at Thy feet
  A student let me be,
And learn, as it is meet,
  My duty, Lord, of Thee;
For Thou didst come on mercy's plan,
And all Thy life was love to man.

Oh! make me as Thou art,
　Thy Spirit, Lord, bestow—
The kind and gentle heart,
　That feels another's woe;
That thus I may be like my Head,
　And in my Saviour's footsteps tread.

PILGRIM OF EARTH.

PILGRIM of earth, who art journeying to
　　heaven!
Heir of Eternal Life! child of the day!
Cared for, watched over, beloved and forgiven—
　Art thou discouraged because of the way?

Cared for, watched over, though often thou
　　seemest
Justly forsaken, nor counted a child;
Loved and forgiven, though rightly thou deemest
　Thyself all unlovely, impure, and defiled.

Weary and thirsty—no water-brook near thee,
　Press on, nor faint at the length of the way;
The God of thy life will assuredly hear thee—
　He will provide thee strength for the day.

Break through the brambles and briers that obstruct thee,
　Dread not the gloom and the blackness of night:

Lean on the Hand that will safely conduct thee—
Trust to His eye to whom darkness is light.

Be trustful, be steadfast, whatever betide thee,
Only one thing do thou ask of the Lord—
Grace to go forward wherever He guide thee,
Simply believing the truth of His word.

Still on thy spirit deep anguish is pressing,
Not for the yoke that His wisdom bestows:
A heavier burden thy soul is distressing,
A heart that is slow in His love to repose.

Earthliness, coldness, unthankful behavior—
Ah! thou mayest sorrow, but do not despair;
Even this grief thou mayest bring to thy Saviour,
Cast upon Him e'en this burden and care!

Bring all thy hardness—His power can subdue it;
How full is the promise! The blessing how free'
" Whatsoever ye ask in my name, I will do it ·
Abide in my love, and be joyful in me."

"WHAT IS THIS THAT HE SAITH: A LITTLE WHILE?"

JOHN 16: 18.

OH! for the peace which floweth as a river,
  Making Life's desert-places bloom and smile
Oh! for a faith to grasp heaven's bright "forever,"
  Amid the shadows of Earth's "little while."

"A little while" for patient vigil-keeping,
  To face the storm, to wrestle with the strong;
"A little while" to sow the seed with weeping,
  Then bind the sheaves and sing the harvest-song

"A little while" to wear the robe of sadness,
  To toil with weary step through erring ways;
Then to pour forth the fragrant oil of gladness,
  And clasp the girdle of the robe of praise.

"A little while" 'mid shadow and illusion,
  To strive by faith Love's mysteries to spell;
Then read each dark enigma's clear solution,
  Then hail Light's verdict—"He doth all things well."

"A little while" the earthen pitcher taking
  To wayside brooks from far-off fountains fed;
Then the parched lip its thirst forever slaking
  Beside the fullness of the Fountain Head.

"A little while" to keep the oil from failing;
  "A little while" Faith's flickering lamp to trim
And then, the Bridegroom's coming footstep hail
      ing,
  To haste to meet Him with the bridal hymn.

And He who is at once both Gift and Giver,
  The future Glory, and the present smile,
With the bright promise of the glad "for ever,"
  Will light the shadows of the "little while."

IN HEAVEN.

"Their angels do always behold the face of my Father."

SILENCE filled the courts of heaven,
  Hushed were seraphs' harp and tone,
When a little new-born seraph
  Knelt before the Eternal Throne;
While its soft, white hands were lifted,
  Clasped as if in earnest prayer,
And its voice, in dove-like murmurs,
  Rose like music on the ear.
Light from the full fount of Glory
  On his robes of whiteness glistened,
And the bright-winged seraphs near Him
  Bowed their radiant heads and listened

"Lord, from Thy Throne of Glory here,
　My heart turns fondly to another ;
O Lord ! our God, the Comforter,
　Comfort. comfort, *my sweet Mother!*
Many sorrows hast Thou sent her,
　Meekly has she drained the cup ;
And the jewels Thou hast lent her,
　Unrepining yielded up :
　　　Comfort, comfort, *my sweet Mother!*

" Earth is growing lonely round her ;
　Friend and lover hast Thou taken ;
Let her not, though woes surround her,
　Feel herself by Thee forsaken.
Let her think, when faint and weary,
　We are waiting for her *here :*
Let each loss that makes earth dreary,
　Make the hope of heaven more dear :
　　　Comfort, comfort, *my sweet Mother!*

" Thou who once, in nature human,
　Dwelt on earth a little child,
Pillowed on the breast of Woman,
　Blessèd Mary ! undefiled.
Thou who, from the cross of suffering,
　Marked Thy Mother's tearful face,
And bequeathed her to Thy loved one,
　Bidding him to fill Thy place :
　　　Comfort, comfort, *my sweet Mother!*

"Thou who once, from heaven descending,
   Tears and woes and conflicts won:
Thou who, nature's laws suspending,
   Gav'st the widow back her son:
Thou who at the grave of Lazarus
   Wept with those who wept their dead:
Thou! who once in mortal anguish
   Bowed Thine own anointed head,
      Comfort, comfort, *my sweet Mother!*"

The dove-like murmurs died away
   Upon the radiant air,
But still the little suppliant knelt
   With hands still clasped in prayer;
Still were those mildly-pleading eyes
   Turned to the sapphire throne,
Till golden harp and angel voice
   Rang forth in mingled tone;
And as the swelling numbers flowed,
   By angel voices given,
Rich, sweet, and clear, the anthem rolled
   Through all the courts of heaven:
"He is the widow's God," it said,
   Who spared not "His own Son,"
The infant cherub bowed his head—
   "Thy will, *O Lord! be done.*"

"IT IS I; BE NOT AFRAID."

MATT. 14 : 37.

TOSSED with rough winds, and faint with fear,
Above the tempest, soft and clear,
What still small accents greet mine ear?
  'Tis I; be not afraid.

" 'Tis I, who led thy steps aright;
'Tis I, who gave thy blind eyes sight;
'Tis I, thy Lord, thy Life, thy Light.
  'Tis I; be not afraid.

" These raging winds, this surging sea,
Bear not a breath of wrath to thee;
That storm has all been spent on me.
  'Tis I; be not afraid.

" This bitter cup fear not to drink;
I know it well—oh! do not shrink;
I tasted it o'er Kedron's brink.
  'Tis I; be not afraid.

Mine eyes are watching by thy bed,
Mine arms are underneath thy head,
My blessing is around thee shed.
  'Tis I; be not afraid.

"When on the other side thy feet
 Shall rest 'mid thousand welcomes sweet,
 One well-known voice thy heart shall greet.
  'Tis I; be not afraid.

"From out the dazzling majesty
 Gently He'll lay His hand on thee,
 Whispering: "Beloved, lov'st thou me?
 'Twas not in vain I died for thee,
  'Tis I; be not afraid."

NATURE AND FAITH.

2 COR. 4 : 17, 18.

WE wept—'twas *Nature* wept, but Faith
 Can pierce beyond the gloom of death,
And in yon world, so fair and bright,
Behold thee in refulgent light!
We miss thee here, yet *Faith* would rather
Know thou art with thy heavenly Father.
 Nature sees the body dead—
 Faith beholds the spirit fled;
 Nature stops at Jordan's tide—
 Faith beholds the other side;
 That but hears farewell and sighs,
 This, thy welcome in the skies;

Nature mourns a *cruel* blow—
Faith assures it is not so;
Nature never sees thee more—
Faith but sees thee gone before;
Nature tells a dismal story—
Faith has visions full of glory;
Nature views the change with sadness—
Faith contemplates it with gladness;
Nature murmurs—Faith gives meekness,
' Strength is perfected in weakness;"
Nature writhes, and hates the rod—
Faith looks up and blesses God;
Sense looks downward—*Faith* above;
That sees harshness – *this* sees love.
Oh! let *Faith* victorious be—
Let it reign triumphantly!

But thou art gone! not lost, but flown!
Shall I then ask thee back, my own,
Back—and leave thy spirit's brightness?
Back—and leave thy robes of whiteness?
Back—and leave thine angel mould?
Back—and leave those streets of gold?
Back—and leave the Lamb who feeds thee?
Back—from founts to which He leads thee?
Back—and leave thy heavenly Father?
Back—to earth and sin?—Nay; rather

Would I live in solitude!
I *would* not ask thee if I *could;*
But patient wait the high decree,
That calls my spirit home to thee!

MY LAMBS.

I LOVED them so,
That when the Elder Shepherd of the fold
Came, covered with the storm, and pale and cold
And begged for one of my sweet lambs to hold,
    I bade him go.

He claimed the pet—
A little fondling thing, that to my breast
Clung always, either in quiet or unrest—
I thought of all my lambs I loved him best,
    And yet—and yet—

I laid him down
In those white, shrouded arms, with bitter tears
For some voice told me that, in after-years,
He should know naught of passion, grief, or fears
    As I had known.

And yet again
That Elder Shepherd came. My heart grew faint

He claimed another lamb, with sadder plaint,
Another! She who, gentle as a saint,
　　Ne'er gave me pain.

　　Aghast I turned away!
There sat she, lovely as an angel's dream,
Her golden locks with sunlight all agleam,
Her holy eyes with heaven in their beam.
　　I knelt to pray.

　　" Is it Thy will?
My Father, say, must this pet lamb be given?
Oh! Thou hast many such, dear Lord, in heaven."
And a soft voice said : " Nobly hast thou striven;
　　But—peace, be still."

　　Oh! how I wept,
And clasped her to my bosom, with a wild
And yearning love—my lamb, my pleasant child
Her, too, I gave. The little angel smiled,
　　And slept.

　　" Go! go!" I cried :
For once again that Shepherd laid His hand
Upon the noblest of our household band.
Like a pale spectre, there He took His stand,
　　Close to his side.

　　And yet how wondrous sweet
The look with which he heard my passionate cry

"Touch not my lamb; for him, oh! let me die!"
"A little while," He said, with smile and sigh,
    "Again to meet."

    Hopeless I fell;
And when I rose, the light had burned so low,
So faint, I could not see my darling go:
He had not bidden me farewell, but oh!
    I felt farewell

    More deeply, far,
Than if my arms had compassed that slight frame:
Though could I but have heard him call my name—
"Dear mother!"—but in heaven 'twill be the same;
    There burns my star!

    He will not take
Another lamb, I thought, for only one
Of the dear fold is spared, to be my sun,
My guide; my mourner when this life is done:
    My heart would break.

    Oh! with what thrill
I heard Him enter! but I did not know
(For it was dark) that He had robbed me so.
The idol of my soul—he could not go—
    O heart! be still!

    Came morning. Can I tell
How this poor frame its sorrowful tenant kept?

For waking tears were mine; I, sleeping, wept,
And days, months, years, that weary vigil kept.
    Alas! " Farewell."

    How often it is said!
I sit and think, and wonder too, sometime,
How it will seem, when, in that happier clime,
It never will ring out like funeral chime
    Over the dead.

    No tears! no tears!
Will there a day come that I shall not weep?
For I bedew my pillow in my sleep:
Yes, yes; thank God! no grief that clime shall
    keep,
    No weary years.

    Ay! it is well:
Well with my lambs, and with their earthly guide
There, pleasant rivers wander they beside,
Or strike sweet harps upon its silver tide—
    Ay! it is well.

    Through the dreary day,
They often come from glorious light to me;
I can not feel their touch, their faces see,
Yet my soul whispers, they do come to me—
    Heaven is not far away.

THE CALL.

THE night was dark; behold, the shade was
    deeper
In the old garden of Gethsemane,
When that calm voice awoke the weary sleeper:
  "Could'st thou not watch one hour alone with
    me?"

O thou! so weary of thy self-denials,
  And so impatient of thy little cross,
Is it so hard to bear thy daily trials,
  To count all earthly things a gainful loss?

What if thou *always* suffer tribulation,
  And if thy Christian warfare never cease,
The gaining of the quiet habitation
  Shall gather thee to everlasting peace.

But here we all must suffer, walking lonely
  The path that Jesus once Himself hath gone:
Watch thou in patience, through the dark hour
    only—
  This one dark hour—before the eternal dawn

The captive's oar may pause upon the galley,
  The soldier sleep beneath his pluméd crest,
And Peace may fold her wings o'er hill and valley;
  But thou, O Christian! must not take thy rest.

Thou must walk on, however man upbraid thee,
　With Him who trod the wine-press all alone;
Thou wilt not find one human hand to aid thee,
　One human soul to comprehend thine own.

Heed not the images forever thronging
　From out the foregone life thou liv'st no more.
Faint-hearted mariner! still art thou longing
　For the dim line of the receding shore?

Wilt thou find rest of soul in thy returning
　To that old path thou hast so vainly trod?
Hast thou forgotten all thy weary yearning
　To walk among the children of thy God:

Faithful and steadfast in their consecration,
　Living by that high faith to thee so dim,
Declaring before God their dedication,
　So far from thee because so near to Him?

Canst thou forget thy Christian superscription,
　" Behold, we count them happy which endure"'
What treasure wouldst thou in the land Egyptian,
　Repass the stormy water to secure?

And wilt thou yield thy sure and glorious promise
　For the poor, fleeting joys earth can afford?
No hand can take away the treasure from us,
　That rests within the keeping of the Lord.

Poor, wandering soul! I know that thou art
    seeking
Some easier way, as all have sought before,
To silence the reproachful inward speaking—
    Some landward path unto an island shore.

The cross is heavy in thy human measure,
    The way too narrow for thine inward pride;
Thou canst not lay thine intellectual treasure
    At the low footstool of the Crucified.

Oh! that my faithless soul, one great hour only,
    Would comprehend the Christian's perfect life,
Despised with Jesus, sorrowful and lonely,
    Yet calmly looking upward in its strife!

For poverty and self-renunciation,
    The Father yielded back a thousand-fold;
In the calm stillness of regeneration,
    Cometh a joy we never knew of old.

In meek obedience to the heavenly Teacher,
    Thy weary soul can find its only peace;
Seeking no aid from any human creature—
    Looking to God alone for his release.

And He will come in His own time and power,
    To set His earnest-hearted children free:
Watch only through this dark and painful hour,
    And the bright morning yet will break for thee.

GOD'S ANVIL.

PAIN'S furnace-heat within me quivers.
  God's breath upon the fire doth blow
And all my heart in anguish shivers,
  And trembles at the fiery glow;
And yet I whisper, "As God will!"
And in His hottest fire hold still.

He comes, and lays my heart, all heated,
  On the bare anvil, minded so
Into His own fair shape to beat it,
  With His great hammer, blow on blow;
And yet I whisper, "As God will!"
And at His heaviest blows hold still.

He takes my softened heart and beats it;
  The sparks fly off at every blow;
He turns it o'er and o'er, and heats it,
  And lets it cool, and makes it glow:
And yet I whisper, "As God will!"
And in His mighty hand hold still.

Why should I murmur? for the sorrow
  Thus only longer-lived would be;
Its end may come, and will, to-morrow,
  When God has done His work in me;

So I say trusting, "As God will!"
And, trusting to the end, hold still.

He kindles, for my profit purely,
　Affliction's glowing, fiery brand;
And all His heaviest blows are surely
　Inflicted by a master-hand;
So I say, praying, "As God will!"
And hope in Him, and suffer still.

THE CROSS AND CROWN.

MUST Jesus bear the cross alone
　And all the world go free?
No; there's a cross for every one,
　And there's a cross for me.

How happy are the saints above,
　Who once went sorrowing here;
But now they taste unmingled love,
　And joy without a tear.

The consecrated cross I'll bear,
　Till death shall set me free;
And then go home, my crown to wear;
　For there's a crown for me.

Upon the crystal pavement, down
  At Jesus' piercéd feet,
Joyful I'll cast my golden crown,
  And His dear name repeat;

And palms shall wave, and harps shall ring
  Beneath heaven's arches high;
The Lord that lives, the ransomed sing,
  That lives no more to die.

EVEN ME.

LORD! I hear of showers of blessing
  Thou art scattering, full and free,
Showers the thirsty soul refreshing—
  Let some droppings fall on me,
            Even me.

Pass me not, O gracious Father!
  Lost and sinful though I be;
Thou mightst curse me, but the rather
  Let Thy mercy light on me,
            Even me.

Pass me not, O tender Saviour!
  Let me love and cling to Thee;

EVEN ME.

Fain I'm longing for Thy favor;
  When Thou callest, call for me,
        Even me.

Pass me not, O mighty Spirit!
  Thou canst make the blind to see;
Testify of Jesus' merit,
  Speak the word of peace to me,
        Even me

Have I long in sin been sleeping,
  Long been slighting, grieving Thee?
Has the world my heart been keeping;
  Oh! forgive and rescue me,
        Even me.

Love of God! so pure and changeless;
  Love of Christ! so rich and free;
Grace of God! so strong and boundless.
  Magnify it all in me,
        Even me.

Pass me not, almighty Spirit!
  Draw this lifeless heart to Thee;
Impute to me the Saviour's merits;
  Blessing others. oh! bless me,
        Even me.

O MY SAVIOUR, CRUCIFIED.

O MY Saviour, crucified!
Near Thy cross may I abide;
There to gaze, with steadfast eye,
On Thy dying agony.

Jesus, bruised and put to shame,
Tells me all the Father's name;
God is love, I surely know,
By my Saviour's depths of woe!

In His sinless soul's distress
I behold my guiltiness;
Oh! how vile my low estate,
Since my ransom was so great.

Dwelling on Mount Calvary,
Contrite shall my spirit be;
Rest and holiness shall find,
Fashioned like my Saviour's mind.

THE PEACE OF GOD.

WE ask for peace, O Lord!
    Thy children ask Thy peace
Not what the world calls rest,
    That toil and care should cease:

That through bright sunny hours,
  Calm life should fleet away,
And tranquil night should fade
    In smiling day.
It is not for such peace that we would pray.

We ask for peace, O Lord!
  Yet not to stand secure,
Girt round with iron pride,
  Contented to endure;
Crushing the gentle strings
  That human hearts should know;
Untouched by others' joys,
    Or others' woe.
Thou, O dear Lord! wilt never teach us so.

We ask Thy peace, O Lord,
  Through storm and fear and strife,
To light and guide us on
  Through a long, struggling life;
While no success or gain
  Shall cheer the desperate fight,
Or nerve what the world calls
    Our wasted might:
Yet pressing through the darkness to the light.

It is Thine own, O Lord!
  Who toil while others sleep;

Who sow, with living care,
  What other hands shall reap;
They lean on Thee, entranced
  In calm and perfect rest;
Give us that peace, O Lord!
  Divine and blest,
Thou keepest for those hearts that love Thee best.

PEACE.

LIFE'S mystery—deep, restless as the ocean—
  Hath surged and wailed for ages to and fro;
Earth's generations watch its ceaseless motion,
  As in and out its hollow moanings flow.
Shivering and yearning by that unknown sea,
Let my soul calm itself, O God! in Thee.

Life's sorrows, with inexorable power,
  Sweep desolation o'er this mortal plain;
And human loves and hopes fly as the chaff
  Borne by the whirlwind from the ripened grain.
Oh! when before that blast my hopes all flee,
Let my soul calm itself, O Christ! in Thee.

Between the mysteries of death and life
  Thou standest, loving, guiding, not explaining

We ask, and Thou art silent; yet we gaze,
  And our charmed hearts forget their drear
    complaining.
No crushing fate, no stony destiny,
Thou "Lamb that hath been slain!" we rest in
    Thee.

The many waves of thought, the mighty tides,
  The ground-swell that rolls up from other lands,
From far-off worlds, from dim, eternal shores;
  Whose echo dashes o'er life's wave-worn strands;
This vague, dark tumult of the inner sea
Grows calm, grows bright, O risen Lord! in Thee.

Thy piercéd hand guides the mysterious wheels,
  Thy thorn-crowned brow now wears the crown
    of power;
And when the dark enigma presseth sore,
  Thy patient voice saith: "Watch with me one
    hour."
As sinks the moaning river in the sea,
In silent peace, so sinks my soul in Thee.

PRAYER FOR STRENGTH.

FATHER! before thy footstool kneeling.
   Once more my heart goes up to Thee
For aid, for strength, to Thee appealing,
   Thou who alone canst succor me.

Hear me! for heart and flesh are failing—
   My spirit yielding in the strife;
And anguish wild, as unavailing,
   Sweeps in a flood across my life.

Help me to stem the tide of sorrow;
   Help me to bear Thy chastening rod;
Give me endurance; let me borrow
   Strength from Thy promise, O my God!

Not mine the grief which words may lighten;
   Not mine the tears of common woe:
The pang with which my heart-strings tighten
   Only the All-seeing One may know.

And I am weak; my feeble spirit
   Shrinks from life's tasks in wild dismay;
Yet not that Thou that task would spare it,
   My Father, do I dare to pray.

Into my soul Thy might infusing,
   Strengthening my spirit by Thine own,

PRAYER FOR STRENGTH.

Help me—all other aid refusing—
   To cling to Thee, and Thee alone.

And oh! in my exceeding weakness,
   Make Thy strength perfect: Thou art strong,
Aid me to do Thy will with meekness,
   Thou to whom all my powers belong.

Saviour! our human form once wearing,
   Help, by the memory of that day,
When, painfully Thy dark cross bearing,
   E'en for a time Thy strength gave way.

Beneath a lighter burden sinking,
   Jesus, I cast myself on Thee;
Forgive, forgive this useless shrinking
   From trials that I know must be.

Oh! let me feel that Thou art near me,
   Close to Thy side I shall not fear:
Hear me, O Strength of Israel! hear me!
   Sustain and aid! in mercy hear!

ONWARD.

TRAVELER, faint not on the road;
  Droop not in the parching sun:
Onward, onward with thy load,
  Till the night be won.
Swerve not, though thy bleeding feet
  Fain the narrow path would leave;
From the burden and the heat
  Thou shalt rest at eve.

'Midst a world that round thee fades,
  Brightening stars and twilight life;
When a sacred calm pervades
  All that now is strife;
Rich the joy to be revealed
  In that hour from labor free,
Bright the splendors that shall yield
  Happiness to thee.

Master of a holy charm,
  Yet be patient on thy way;
Use the spell and check the harm
  That would lead astray.
From the petty cares that teem,
  Turn thee with prophetic eye,
To the glory of that dream
  Which shall never die.

By the mystery of thy trust;
  By the grandeur of that hour
When mortality and dust
  Clothed eternal power;
By the purple robe of shame,
  The mockery, and the insulting rod,
By the anguish that o'ercame
  The incarnate God:

Faint not! fail not! be thou strong,
  Cast away distrust and fear;
Though the weary day seems long,
  Yet the night is near.
Friends and kindred wait beyond—
  They who passed the trial pure:
Traveler, by that holy bond,
  Shrink not to endure.

GRIEF WAS SENT THEE FOR THY GOOD

SOME there are who seem exempted
  From the doom incurred by all;
Are they not more sorely tempted?
  Are they not the first to fall?
As a mother's firm denial
  Checks her infant's wayward mood,
Wisdom lurks in every trial—
  Grief was sent thee for thy good.

In the scenes of former pleasure,
  Present anguish hast thou felt;
O'er thy fond heart's dearest treasure,
  As a mourner hast thou knelt;
In thy hour of deep affliction,
  Let no impious thoughts intrude:
Meekly bow, with this conviction—
  Grief was sent thee for thy good.

SCENES "ON JORDAN'S STRAND."

THERE came a little child, with sunny hair,
  All fearless to the brink of Death's dark river,
And with a sweet confiding in the care
  Of Him who is of life the Joy and Giver;
And as upon the waves she left our sight,
  We heard her say: "My Saviour makes them bright."

Next came a youth, with bearing most serene,
  Nor turned a single backward look of sadness;
But, as he left each gay and flowery scene,
  Smiling declared: "My soul is thrilled with gladness!

What earth deems bright, forever I resign,
  Joyful but this to know, that Christ is mine."

An aged mourner, trembling, tottered by,
  And paused a moment by the swelling river,
Then glided on beneath the shadowy sky,
  Singing: "Christ Jesus is my strength forever
Upon His arm my feeble soul I lean,
My glance meets His, without a cloud between."

And scarce her last triumphant note had died,
  Ere hastened on a man of wealth and learning,
Who cast at once his bright renown aside,
  These only words to his friends returning:
"Christ for my Wisdom thankfully I own,
And as 'a little child' I seek His throne."

Then saw I this: that, whether guileless child,
  Or youth, or age, or genius, won salvation,
Each self-renouncing came; on each God smiled;
  Each found the love of Christ rich compensation
For loss of friends, earth's pleasures and renown;
Each entered heaven, and "by His side sat down."

THERE IS LIGHT BEYOND.

BEYOND the stars that shine in golden glory,
　　Beyond the calm sweet moon,
Up the bright ladder saints have trod before thee,
　　Soul! thou shalt venture soon.
Secure with Him who sees thy heart-sick yearning,
　　Safe in His arms of love,
Thou shalt exchange the midnight for the morning
　　And thy fair home above.

Oh! it is sweet to watch the world's night wearing,
　　The Sabbath morn come on,
And sweet it were the vineyard labor sharing—
　　Sweeter the labor done.
All finished! all the conflict and the sorrow,
　　Earth's dream of anguish o'er;
Deathless there dawns for thee a nightless morrow
　　On Eden's blissful shore.

Patience! then, patience! soon the pang of dying
　　Shall all forgotten be,
And thou, through rolling spheres rejoicing, flying
　　Beyond the waveless sea,

Shalt know hereafter where thy Lord doth lead
   thee,
  His darkest dealings trace,
And by those fountains where His love will feed
   thee,
  Behold Him face to face.

Then bow thine head, and God shall give thee
   meekness,
  Bravely to do His will;
So shall arise His glory in thy weakness—
  O struggling soul! be still.
Dark clouds are His pavilion shining o'er thee,
  Thine heart must recognize
The veiled Shechinah moving on before thee,
  Too bright to meet thine eyes.

Behold the wheel that straightly moves, and
   fleetly
  Performs the Sovereign Word;
Thou know'st His suffering love! then suffering
   meekly,
  Follow thy loving Lord!
Watch on the tower, and listen by the gateway,
  Nor weep to wait alone;
Take thou thy spices, and some angel straightway
  Shall roll away the stone.

Then shalt thou tell thy living Lord hath risen,
    And risen but to save;
Tell of the might that breaks the Captive's prison
    And life beyond the grave!
Tell how He met thee, all His radiance shrouded;
    How in thy sorrow came
His pitying voice breathing, when faith was clouded,
    Thine own familiar name.

So at the grave's dark portal thou may'st linger,
    And hymn some happy strain;
The passing world may mock the feeble singer—
    Heed not, but sing again.
Thus wait, thus watch, till He the last link sever,
    And changeless rest be won;
Then in His glory thou shalt bask forever,
    Fear not the clouds—PRESS ON!

"THY WILL BE DONE!"

FOUR little words—no more—
    Easy to say,
But thoughts that went before,
    Can words convey?

"THY WILL BE DONE."

The struggle, only known
  To one proud soul,
And Him whose eye alone
  Has marked the whole.

Before that stubborn will
  At length was broke,
And a low " Peace, be still,"
  One soft Voice spoke;

The pang, when that sad heart
  Its dreams resigned,
And strength was found, to part
  Those bonds long twined,

To yield that treasure up,
  So fondly clasped,
To drain that bitter cup,
  So sadly grasped!

But all is calm at last,
  "Thy will be done!"
Enough, the storm is past,
  The field is won.

Now for the peaceful breast,
  The quiet sleep;
For soul and spirit rest,
  Tranquil and deep.

Rest, whose full bliss and power
  They only know
Who knew the bitter hour
  Of restless woe.

The rebel will subdued—
  The fond heart free—
"Thy will be done!"—*all* good
  That comes from Thee.

All weary thought and care,
  Lord, we resign;
Ours is to do, to bear,
  To choose is Thine.

Four little words—no more—
  Easy to say;
But what was felt before,
  Can words convey?

THEY SHALL BE MINE!

"THEY shall be mine!" Oh! lay them down to slumber,
Calm in the strong assurance that He gives;
He calls them by their names, He knows their number,
And they shall live as surely as He lives.

"They shall be mine!" upraised from earthly
    pillows,
  Gathered from desert sand, from mountains
    cold—
Called from the graves beneath old ocean's bil-
    lows,
  Called from each distant land, each scattered
    fold.

Well might the soul, that wondrous spark of
    being,
  Lit by His breath who claims it for His own,
Shine in the circle which His love foreseeing,
  Destined to glitter brightest by His throne.

But shall the dust from earthly dust first taken,
  And now long mingled with its native earth,
To life, to beauty, once again awaken,
  Thrill with the rapture of a second birth?

"They shall be mine!" they, as on earth we knew
    them—
  The lips we kissed, the hands we loved to press—
Only a fuller life be circling through them,
  Unfading youth, unchanging holiness.

"They shall be mine!" children of sin and sorrow
  Giv'st Thou, O Lord' heaven's almost verge to
    them?

Not from each rifled grave Thy crown shall borrow
  An added light—a prized and costly gem.

'They shall be mine!" Thought fails, and feeling
    falters,
  Striving to sound and fathom love divine;
All that we know—no time Thy promise alters—
  All that we trust, our loved ones shall be Thine.

LEAVE ME NOT NOW.

LEAVE me not now, while still the shade is
    creeping
  O'er the sad heart that longs to rest in Thee;
Hear my complaint, and while my soul is weeping,
  Breathe Thou the holy dew of sympathy.

Leave me not now, Thou Saviour of compassion,
  While yet the busy tempter lurketh near:
Lord, by Thine anguish and Thy wondrous passion
  Do I entreat Thee now to linger here.

Jesus, Thou soul of love, Thou heart of feeling,
  Let me repose the weary night away
Safe on Thy bosom, all my woes revealing,
  Secure from danger, till the dawn of day.

Then leave me not, O Comforter, and Father,
  Parent of love! I live but in Thy sight;
Good Shepherd, to Thy fold the wand'rer gather
  There to adore Thee, morning, noon, and night.

FAITH'S REPOSE.

FATHER, beneath Thy sheltering wing
  In sweet security we rest,
And fear no evil earth can bring,
  In life, in death, supremely blest.

For life is good, whose tidal flow
  The motions of Thy will obeys;
And death is good, that makes us know
  The Love Divine that all things sways.

And good it is to bear the cross
  And so Thy perfect peace to win;
And naught is ill, nor brings us loss,
  Nor works us harm, save only sin.

Redeemed from this, we ask no more,
  But trust the love that saves to guide—
The grace that yields so rich a store,
  Will grant us all we need beside.

THE DELECTABLE MOUNTAINS.

I SEE them far away,
   In their calm beauty on the evening skies,
Across the golden west their summits rise,
   Bright with the radiance of departing day.
And often, ere the sunset light was gone,
Gazing and longing, I have hastened on,
As with new strength, all weariness and pain
Forgotten in the hope those blissful heights to
   gain.

   Heaven lies not far beyond,
But these are hills of earth, our changeful air
Circles around them, and the dwellers there
   Still own mortality's mysterious bond.
The ceaseless contact, the continued strife,
Of sin and grace, which can but close with life,
Is not yet ended, and the Jordan's roar
Still sounds between their path and the Celestial
   shore.

   But there, the pilgrims say,
On these calm heights, the tumult and the noise
Of all our busy cares and restless joys
   Has almost in the distance died away;
All the past journey "a right way" appears,
Thoughts of the future wake no faithless fears,

And through the clouds, to their rejoicing eyes,
The city's golden streets and pearly gates arise.

Courage, poor fainting heart!
These happy ones in the far distance seen,
Were sinful wanderers once, as thou hast been,
  Weary and sorrowful, as now thou art.
Linger no longer on the lonely plain,
Press boldly onward, and thou too shalt gain
Their vantage-ground, and then with vigor new,
All thy remaining race and pilgrimage pursue.

Ah! far too faint, too poor
Are all our views and aims—we only stand
Within the borders of the promised land,
  Its precious things we seek not to secure,
And thus our hands hang down, and oft unstrung
Our harps are left the willow-trees among;
Lord, lead us forward, upward, till we know
How much of heavenly bliss may be enjoyed below.

"And then, said they, we will, if the day be clear, show you the Delectable Mountains. . . . . So he looked, and behold, at a great distance he saw a most pleasant mountainous country, ... very delectable to behold, ... and it is as common, said they. as this hill is, to and for all the pilgrims. And when thou comest there from thence thou mayest see to the gates of the Celestial City."– *Bunyan.*

THE ANCHOR WITHIN THE VEIL.

AMID the shadows and the fears
That overcloud this home of tears,
Amid my poverty and sin,
The tempest and the war within,
    I cast my soul on Thee,
    Mighty to save e'en me,
    Jesus, Thou Son of God!

Drifting across a sunless sea,
Cold, heavy mist, encurtaining me;
Toiling along life's broken road,
With snares around, and foes abroad,
    I cast my soul on Thee,
    Mighty to save e'en me,
    Jesus, Thou Son of God!

Mine is a day of fear and strife,
A needy soul, a needy life,
A needy world, a needy age;
Yet in my perilous pilgrimage,
    I cast my soul on Thee,
    Mighty to save e'en me,
    Jesus, Thou Son of God!

To Thee I come—ah! only Thou
Canst wipe the sweat from off this brow;
Thou, only Thou, canst make me whole,
And soothe the fever of my soul;
  I cast my soul on Thee,
  Mighty to save e'en me,
  Jesus, Thou Son of God!

On Thee I rest—Thy love and grace
Are my sole rock and resting-place:
In Thee my thirst and hunger sore,
Lord, let me quench for evermore.
  I cast my soul on Thee,
  Mighty to save e'en me,
  Jesus, Thou Son of God!

'Tis earth, not heaven; 'tis night, not noon
The sorrowless is coming soon;
But till the morn of love appears,
Which ends the travail and the tears,
  I cast my soul on Thee,
  Mighty to save e'en me,
  Jesus, Thou Son of God!

GOD'S WAYS.

HOW few who from their youthful day
Look on to what their life may be,
Painting the visions of the way
In colors soft, and bright, and free;
How few who to such paths have brought
The hopes and dreams of early thought!
For God, through ways they have not known,
Will lead His own.

The eager hearts, the souls of fire
Who pant to toil for God and man,
And view with eyes of keen desire
The upland way of toil and pain;
Almost with scorn they think of rest,
Of holy calm, of tranquil breast;
But God, through ways they have not known,
Will lead His own.

A lowlier task on them is laid,
With love to make the labor light;
And then their beauty they must shed,
On quiet homes and lost to sight.
Changed are their visions high and fair,
Yet calm and still they labor there;
For God through ways they have not known,
Will lead His own.

The gentle heart that thinks with pain
    It scarce can lowliest tasks fulfil,
And if it dared its life to scan
    Would ask but pathway low and still;
Often such lowly heart is brought
    To act with power beyond its thought;
For God, through ways they have not known,
    Will lead His own.

And they the bright, who long to prove
    In joyous path, in cloudless lot,
How fresh from earth their grateful love
    Can spring without a stain or spot;
Often such youthful heart is given
The path of grief to walk to heaven;
For God, through ways they have not known,
    Will lead His own.

What matter what the path shall be?
    The end is clear and bright to view:
He knows that we a strength shall see
    Whate'er the day shall bring to do:
We see the end, the house of God,
But not the path to that abode;
For God, through ways they have not known,
    Will lead His own.

DISTRACTIONS IN PRAYER.

I CAN NOT pray; yet, Lord, thou know'st
  The pain it is to me,
To have my vainly struggling thoughts
  Thus torn away from Thee.

Prayer was not meant for luxury
  Of selfish pastime sweet;
It is the prostrate creature's place
  At his Creator's feet.

Had I, dear Lord, no pleasure found
  But in the thoughts of Thee,
Prayer would have come unsought, and been
  A truer liberty.

Yet Thou art oft most present, Lord,
  In weak distracted prayer;
A sinner out of heart with self
  Most often finds Thee there.

And prayer that humbles, sets the soul
  From all illusions free,
And teaches it how utterly,
  Dear Lord, it hangs on Thee.

The soul that on self-sacrifice
   Is dutifully bent,
Will bless the chastening hand that makes
   Its prayer its punishment.

Ah, Jesus! why should I complain?
   And why fear aught but sin?
Distractions are but outward things;
   Thy peace dwells far within!

These surface troubles come and go
   Like rufflings of the sea;
The deeper depth is out of reach
   To all, my God, but Thee!

MY GUEST.

I HAVE a wonderful Guest,
   Who speeds my feet, who moves my hand,
Who strengthens, comforts, guides, commands,
   Whose presence gives me rest.

He dwells within my soul;
He swept away the filth and gloom,
He garnished fair the empty room,
   And now pervades the whole.

MY GUEST.

For aye, by day and night,
He keeps the portals—suffers naught
Defile the temple He has bought,
   And filled with joy and light.

Once 'twas a cavern dim;
The home of evil thoughts, desires,
Enkindled by infernal fires,
   Without one thought of Him.

Regenerated by His grace,
Still 'tis a meagre inn, at best.
Wherein the King's to make His rest.
   And show His glorious face.

Yet, Saviour, ne'er depart
From this poor earthly cottage home
Until the Father bid me come,
   Whisp'ring within my heart:

" I shake these cottage walls;
Fear not! at My command they bow,
My heavenly mansions open now,
   As this poor dwelling falls."

Then my dear wondrous Guest
Shall bear me on His own right hand
Unto that fair and Promised Land,
   Where I in Him shall rest.

COMING.

"At even, or at midnight, or at the cock-crowing, or in the morning."

" IT may be in the evening,
  When the work of the day is done,
And you have time to sit in the twilight
  And watch the sinking sun,
While the long bright day dies slowly
  Over the sea,
And the hour grows quiet and holy
  With thoughts of me;
While you hear the village children
  Passing along the street,
Among those thronging footsteps
  May come the sound of *my* feet.
Therefore I tell you: Watch
  By the light of the evening star,
When the room is growing dusky
  As the clouds afar;
Let the door be on the latch
  In your home,
For it may be through the gloaming
  I will come.

" It may when the midnight
  Is heavy upon the land,

And the black waves lying dumbly
    Along the sand;
When the moonless night draws close,
And the lights are out in the house
When the fires burn low and red.
And the watch is ticking loudly
    Beside the bed:
Though you sleep, tired out, on your couch,
Still your heart must wake and watch
    In the dark room,
For it may be that at midnight
    I will come.

" It may be at the cock-crow,
When the night is dying slowly
    In the sky,
And the sea looks calm and holy,
    Waiting for the dawn
    Of the golden sun
    Which draweth nigh;
When the mists are on the valleys, shading
    The rivers chill,
And my morning-star is fading, fading
    Over the hill:
Behold I say unto you: Watch;
Let the door be on the latch
    In your home;
In the chill before the dawning,

Between the night and morning,
    I may come.

"It may be in the morning,
    When the sun is bright and strong,
And the dew is glittering sharply
    Over the little lawn;
When the waves are laughing loudly
    Along the shore,
And the little birds are singing sweetly
    About the door;
With the long day's work before you,
    You rise up with the sun,
And the neighbors come in to talk a little
    Of all that must be done:
But remember that *I* may be the next
    To come in at the door,
To call you from all your busy work
    For evermore:
As you work your heart must watch,
    For the door is on the latch
    In your room,
And it may be in the morning
    I will come."

So He passed down my cottage garden,
    By the path that leads to the sea,

Till He came to the turn of the little road
    Where the birch and laburnum tree
Lean over and arch the way;
There I saw Him a moment stay,
    And turn once more to me,
    As I wept at the cottage door,
And lift up His hands in blessing—
    Then I saw His face no more.

And I stood still in the doorway,
    Leaning against the wall,
Not heeding the fair white roses,
    Though I crushed them and let them fall
Only looking down the pathway,
    And looking toward the sea,
And wondering, and wondering
    When He would come back for me;
Till I was aware of an Angel
    Who was going swiftly by,
With the gladness of one who goeth
    In the light of God Most High.

He passed the end of the cottage
    Toward the garden gate—
(I suppose he was come down
At the setting of the sun

To comfort some one in the village
    Whose dwelling was desolate)—
And he paused before the door
    Beside my place,
And the likeness of a smile
    Was on his face :
"Weep not," he said, "for unto you is given
    To watch for the coming of His feet
Who is the glory of our blessed heaven ;
    The work and watching will be very
      sweet,
    Even in an earthly home ;
And in such an hour as you think not
    He will come."

So I am watching quietly
    Every day.
Whenever the sun shines brightly,
    I rise and say :
"Surely it is the shining of His face!"
    And look unto the gates of His high place
      Beyond the sea ;
For I know He is coming shortly
    To summon me.
And when a shadow falls across the window
    Of my room,
Where I am working my appointed task,

I lift my head to watch the door and ask
    If He is come;
And the Angel answers sweetly
    In my home :
" Only a few more shadows,
    And He will come."

A QUIET MIND.

I HAVE a treasure which I prize;
    Its like I can not find :
There's nothing like it on the earth ;
    'Tis this—a quiet mind.

But 'tis not that I'm stupefied,
    Or senseless, dull, or blind;
'Tis God's own peace within my heart,
    Which forms my quiet mind.

I found this treasure at the cross :
    And there to every kind
Of weary, heavy-laden souls
    Christ gives a quiet mind.

My Saviour's death and risen life
    To give it were designed :
His love, the never-failing spring
    Of this, my quiet mind.

A QUIET MIND.

The love of God within my breast,
  My heart to Him doth bind;
This is the peace of heaven on earth—
  This is my quiet mind.

I've many a cross to take up now,
  And many left behind;
But present troubles move me not,
  Nor shake my quiet mind.

And what may be to-morrow's cross,
  I never seek to find;
My Saviour says: "Leave that to me,
  And keep a quiet mind."

And well I know the Lord hath said,
  To make my heart resigned,
That mercy still shall follow those
  Who have this quiet mind.

I meet with pride of wit and wealth,
  And scorn, and looks unkind;
It matters not—I envy none,
  While I've a quiet mind.

I'm waiting now to see my Lord,
  So patient and so kind;
I want to thank Him face to face,
  For this my quiet mind.

ALL IS LIGHT.

WHAT though storm-clouds gather round me,
  Hovering darkly o'er my way?
While I see the cross of Calvary
  Beaming with celestial ray,
    All is light, all is light!

What though mortal powers may falter?
  Earthly plans and prospects fail?
With a heaven-born hope which entereth
  E'en to that within the veil,
    All is light, all is light!

What though all my future pathway
  Be from mortal sight concealed?
With the love of Jesus glowing,
  As it lies to faith revealed,
    All is light, all is light!

E'en though death's deep vale before me
  Seem o'erspread with thickest gloom,
While I see a heavenly radiance
  Bursting from beyond the tomb,
    All is light, all is light!

LONGINGS.

WHEN shall I be at rest? My trembling heart
Grows weary of its burden, sickening still
With hopes deferred. Oh! that it were Thy will
To loose my bonds, and take me where Thou art.

When shall I be at rest? My eyes grow dim
　With straining through the gloom; I scarce can see
　The waymarks that my Saviour left for me.
Would it were morn, and I were safe with Him!

When shall I be at rest? Hand over hand
　I grasp, and climb an ever steeper hill,
　A rougher path. Oh! that it were Thy will
My tired feet might tread the Promised Land!

Oh! that I were at rest! A thousand fears
　Come thronging o'er me, lest I fall at last.
　Would I were safe, all toil and danger past,
And Thine own hands might wipe away my tears.

Oh! that I were at rest, like some I love,
Whose last fond looks drew half my life away
Seeming to plead that either they might stay
With me on earth, or I with them above.

But why these murmurs? Thou didst never shrink
From any toil or weariness for me—
Not even from that last deep agony.
Shall I beneath my little trials sink?

No, Lord ; for when I am indeed at rest,
One taste of that deep bliss will quite efface
The sternest memories of my earthly race,
Save but to swell the sense of being blest.

Then lay on me whatever cross I need
To bring me there. I know Thou canst not be
Unkind, unfaithful, or untrue to me!
Shall I not toil for Thee, when Thou for me didst bleed?

BRIDGES.

I HAVE a bridge within my heart,
  Known as the Bridge of Sighs;
It stretches from life's sunny part,
  To where its darkness lies.

And when upon this bridge I stand,
  To watch life's tide below,
Sad thoughts come from the shadowy land
  And darken all its flow.

Then, as it winds its way along
  To sorrow's bitter sea,
Oh! mournful is the spirit-song
  That upward floats to me.

A song which breathes of blessings dead,
  Of friends and friendships flown;
And pleasures gone!—their distant tread
  Now to an echo grown.

And hearing thus, beleaguering fears
  Soon shut the present out,
While joy but in the past appears,
  And in the future doubt.

Oh! often then will deeper grow
  The night that round me lies;
I wish that life had run its flow,
  Or never found its rise!

I have a bridge within my heart,
   Known as the Bridge of Faith;
It spans, by a mysterious art,
   The streams of life and death.

And when upon this bridge I stand,
   To watch the tide below,
Sweet thoughts come from the sunny land
   And brighten all its flow.

Then, as it winds its way along
   Down to a distant sea,
Oh! pleasant is the spirit-song
   That upward floats to me.

A song of blessings never sere,
   Of love "beyond compare,"
Of pleasures flowed from troublings here
   To rise serenely there.

And, hearing thus, a peace divine
   Soon shuts each sorrow out;
And all is hopeful and benign,
   Where all was fear and doubt.

Oh! often then will brighter grow
   The light that round me lies;
I see from life's beclouded flow
   A crystal stream arise.

"FATHER, TAKE MY HAND."

THE way is dark, my Father! Cloud on cloud
Is gathering thickly o'er my head, and loud
The thunders roar above me. See, I stand
Like one bewildered! Father, take my hand,
      And through the gloom
      Lead safely home
        Thy child!

The day goes fast, my Father! and the night
Is drawing darkly down. My faithless sight
Sees ghostly visions. Fears, a spectral band,
Encompass me. O Father! take my hand,
      And from the night
      Lead up to light
        Thy child!

The way is long, my Father! and my soul
Longs for the rest and quiet of the goal:
While yet I journey through this weary land,
Keep me from wandering. Father, take my hand
      Quickly and straight
      Lead to heaven's gate
        Thy child!

The path is rough, my Father! Many a thorn
Has pierced me; and my weary feet, all torn
And bleeding, mark the way. Yet Thy command
Bids me press forward. Father, take my hand;
    Then, safe and blest,
      Lead up to rest
        Thy child!

The throng is great, my Father! Many a doubt
And fear and danger compass me about:
And foes oppress me sore. I can not stand
Or go alone. O Father! take my hand,
    And through the throng
      Lead safe along
        Thy child!

The cross is heavy, Father! I have borne
It long, and still do bear it. Let my worn
And fainting spirit rise to that blest land
Where crowns are given. Father, take my hand
    And, reaching down,
      Lead to the crown
        Thy child!

THE GRACIOUS ANSWER.

The way is dark, my child! but leads to light;
I would not always have thee walk by sight.
My dealings now, thou canst not understand.
I meant it so; but I will take thy hand,
   And through the gloom
   Lead safely home
    My child!

The day goes fast, my child! But is the night
Darker to me than day? In me is light!
Keep close to me, and every spectral band
Of fears shall vanish. I will take thy hand,
   And through the night
   Lead up to light
    My child!

The way is long, my child! But it shall be
Not one step longer than is best for thee;
And thou shalt know, at last, when thou shalt stand
Safe at the goal, how I did take thy hand,
   And quick, and straight
   Lead to heaven's gate
    My child!

THE GRACIOUS ANSWER.

*The path is rough, my child! But oh! how sweet
Will be the rest, for weary pilgrims meet,
When thou shalt reach the borders of that land
To which I lead thee, as I take thy hand;
    And safe and blest
    With me shalt rest
      My child!*

*The throng is great, my child! But at thy side
Thy Father walks: then be not terrified:
For I am with thee; will thy foes command
To let thee freely pass; will take thy hand,
    And through the throng
    Lead safe along
      My child!*

*The cross is heavy, child! Yet there was One
Who bore a heavier for thee: my Son,
My Well-beloved. For Him bear thine; and stand
With Him at last; and, from thy Father's hand,
    Thy cross laid down,
    Receive a crown,
      My child!*

ASLEEP ON GUARD!

"O SHAME!" we're sometimes fain to say,
"On Peter sleeping, while his dear Lord lay
Awake with anguish, in the garden's shade,
Waiting His hour to be betrayed."

We say, or think, if we had gone
Thither—instead of Peter, James, and John—
And Christ had left us on the outpost dim,
As sentinels, to watch with Him;

We would have sooner died, than sleep
The little time we vigil had to keep;
Then wake, to feel His torturing question's power:
"Could ye not watch with me one hour?"

One hour in sad Gethsemane!
And such an hour as that to Him must be!
All night our tireless eyes had pierced the shade
Where He in grief's great passion prayed.

What do we now, to make our word
Seem no vain boast of love to Christ our Lord?
We can not take the chidden sleeper's place,
And shun, by proof, his deep disgrace!

No more, the olive's shade beneath,
The human Christ foretastes the cup of death,
And leaves His servants in the outer gloom,
To watch till He again shall come!

Yet are there midnights dark and dread,
When Jesus still by traitors is betrayed;
Our bosom-sin's the lurking foe at hand,
And "Watch with me" is Christ's command.

One little hour of sleepless care,
And sin could wrest no victory from us there,
But, with the fame of our loved Lord to keep,
Like those we scorn, we fall asleep.

Oh! if our risen Lord must chide
Our souls, for slumbering His death-cross beside,
What face have we to boast our feeble sense
Had shamed poor Peter's vigilance!

On Peter, James, and John, no more
The wrong reproach of hasty pride we pour;
But feel within the question's torturing power,
"Could *ye* not watch with me one hour?"

THE HOUR OF PRAYER.

MY God, is any hour so sweet,
   From blush of morn to evening star,
As that which calls me to Thy feet—
   The hour of prayer!

Blest is that tranquil hour of morn,
   And blest that hour of solemn eve,
When, on the wings of faith up-borne,
   The world I leave!

For then a day-spring shines on me,
   Brighter than morn's ethereal glow;
And richer dews descend from Thee
   Than earth can know.

Then is my strength by Thee renewed;
   Then do I feel my sins forgiven;
Then dost Thou cheer my solitude
   With joys of heaven.

No words can tell what sweet relief
   There for my every want I find;
What strength for warfare, balm for grief,
   What peace of mind.

Hushed is each doubt, gone every fear;
My spirit seems in heaven to stay;
And even the penitential tear
   Is wiped away.

Lord! till I reach that blissful shore,
No privilege so dear shall be,
As thus my inmost soul to pour
   In prayer to Thee.

THY WILL BE DONE.

WE see not, know not. All our way
   Is night. With Thee alone is day.
From out the torrent's troubled drift,
Above the storm—our prayers we lift—
   Thy will be done!

The flesh may fail, the heart may faint,
But who are we, to make complaint,
Or dare to plead, in times like these,
The weakness of our love of ease?
   Thy will be done!

We take with solemn thankfulness
Our burden up, nor ask it less;
And count it joy that even we

May suffer, serve, or wait for Thee,
    Whose will be done!

Though dim, as yet, in tint and line,
We trace Thy picture's wise design,
And thank Thee that our age supplies
Its dark relief of sacrifice—
    Thy will be done!

And if, in our unworthiness,
Thy sacrificial wine we press;
If, from Thy ordeal's heated bars,
Our feet are seamed with crimson scars,
    Thy will be done!

If, for the age to come, this hour
Of trial hath vicarious power;
And, blest by Thee, our present pain
Be Liberty's eternal gain,
    Thy will be done!

Strike! Thou the Master, we Thy keys,
The anthem of the destinies!
The minor of Thy loftier strain,
Our hearts shall breathe the old refrain—
    Thy will be done!

HYMN OF TRUST.

O LOVE Divine! that stooped to share
  Our sharpest pang, our bitterest tear;
On Thee we cast each earth-born care;
  We smile at pain while Thou art near!

Though long the weary way we tread,
  And sorrows crown each lingering year,
No path we shun, no darkness dread,
  Our hearts still whispering, Thou art near.

When drooping pleasure turns to grief,
  And trembling faith is changed to fear,
The murmuring wind, the quivering leaf,
  Shall softly tell us, Thou art near!

On Thee we fling our burdening woe,
  O Love Divine! forever dear;
Content to suffer, while we know,
  Living, and dying, Thou art near!

THE BURIAL OF MOSES.

BY Nebo's lonely mountain,
   On this side Jordan's wave.
In a vale in the land of Moab,
   There lies a lonely grave;
And no man dug that sepulchre,
   And no man saw it e'er,
For the "Sons of God" upturned the sod,
   And laid the dead man there.

That was the grandest funeral
   That ever passed on earth;
But no man heard the trampling,
   Or saw the train go forth.
Noiselessly as the day-light
   Comes when the night is done,
And the crimson streak on ocean's cheek
   Grows into the great sun—

Noiselessly as the spring-time
   Her crown of verdure weaves,
And all the trees on all the hills
   Open their thousand leaves;

So, without sound of music,
 Or voice of them that wept,
Silently down from the mountain's crown
 The great procession swept.

Perchance the bald old eagle,
 On gray Beth-peor's height,
Out of his rocky eyry
 Looked on the wondrous sight;
Perchance the lion stalking,
 Still shuns that hallowed spot:
For beast and bird have seen and heard
 That which man knoweth not.

But when the warrior dieth,
 His comrades in the war,
With arms reversed, and muffled drum,
 Follow the funeral car.
They show the banners taken,
 They tell his battles won,
And after him lead his masterless steed,
 While peals the minute-gun.

Amid the noblest of the land
 Men lay the sage to rest,
And give the bard an honored place,
 With costly marble drest—

In the great minster transept,
   Where lights like glories fall,
And the sweet choir sings, and the organ rings
   Along the emblazoned wall.

This was the bravest warrior
   That ever buckled sword;
This, the most gifted poet
   That ever breathed a word;
And never earth's philosopher
   Traced with his golden pen,
On the deathless page, truths half so sage
   As he wrote down for men.

And had he not high honor?
   The hill-side for his pall,
To lie in state while angels wait,
   With stars for tapers tall,
And the dark rock-pines like tossing plumes
   Over his bier to wave,
And God's own hand, in that lonely land,
   To lay him in the grave!

In that deep grave without a name,
   Whence his uncoffined clay
Shall break again—most wondrous thought—
   Before the Judgment-day,

And stand, with glory wrapped around,
  On the hills he never trod,
And speak of the strife that won our life
  With the Incarnate Son of God.

O lonely tomb in Moab's land !
  O dark Beth-peor hill !
Speak to these curious hearts of ours,
  And teach them to be still.
God hath His mysteries of grace,
  Ways that we can not tell;
And hides them deep, like the secret sleep
  Of him He loved so well.

"NOW."

"RISE ! for the day is passing,
  And you lie dreaming on ;
The others have buckled their armor,
  And forth to the fight are gone :
A place in the ranks awaits you,
  Each man has some part to play;
The Past and the Future are looking
  In the face of the stern To-day.

THE NEED OF JESUS.

I NEED Thee, precious Jesus,
   For I am full of sin;
My soul is dark and guilty,
   My heart is dead within;
I need the cleansing fountain,
   Where I can always flee—
The blood of Christ most precious,
   The sinner's perfect plea.

I need Thee, precious Jesus'
   For I am very poor;
A stranger and a pilgrim,
   I have no earthly store;
I need the love of Jesus,
   To cheer me on my way:
To guide my doubting footsteps
   To be my strength and stay.

I need Thee, precious Jesus!
   I need a friend like Thee—
A friend to soothe and sympathize
   A friend to care for me;
I need the heart of Jesus,
   To feel each anxious care,
To tell my every want,
   And all my sorrows share.

THE NEED OF JESUS.

I need Thee, precious Jesus,
   For I am very blind;
A weak and foolish wanderer,
   With a dark and evil mind;
I need the light of Jesus,
   To tread the thorny road,
To guide me safe to glory—
   Where I shall see my God.

I need Thee, precious Jesus!
   I need Thee day by day—
To fill me with Thy fulness,
   To lead me on my way;
I need Thy Holy Spirit,
   To teach me what I am,
To show me more of Jesus,
   To point me to the Lamb.

I need Thee, precious Jesus!
   And hope to see Thee soon,
Encircled with the rainbow,
   And seated on Thy throne;
There, with Thy blood-bought children,
   My joy shall ever be,
To sing Thy praises, Jesus!
   To gaze, my Lord, on Thee!

THE CHRISTIAN AND HIS ECHO.

TRUE faith, producing love to God and man,
Say, Echo, is not this the Gospel plan?
    The Gospel plan.

Must I my faith and love to Jesus show,
By doing good to all, both friend and foe?
    Both friend and foe.

But if a brother hates and treats me ill,
Must I return him good, and love him still?
    Love him still.

If he my failings watches to reveal,
Must I his faults as carefully conceal?
    As carefully conceal.

But if my name and character he blast,
And cruel malice, too, a long time last;
And, if I sorrow and affliction know,
He loves to add unto my cup of woe;
In this uncommon, this peculiar case,
Sweet Echo, say, must I still love and bless?
    Still love and bless.

Whatever usage ill I may receive,
Must I be patient still, and still forgive?
    Be patient still, and still forgive.

THE CHRISTIAN AND HIS ECHO.

Why, Echo, how is this? thou'rt sure a dove!
Thy voice shall teach me nothing else but love!
    Nothing else but love.

Amen! with all my heart, then be it so;
'Tis all delightful, just, and good, I know:
And now to practise I'll directly go.
    Directly go.

Things being so, whoever me reject,
My gracious God me surely will protect.
    Surely will protect.

Henceforth I'll roll on Him my every care,
And then both friend and foe embrace in prayer.
    Embrace in prayer.

But after all those duties I have done,
Must I, in point of merit, them disown,
And trust for heaven through Jesus' blood alone?
    Through Jesus' blood alone.

Echo, enough! thy counsels to mine ear
Are sweeter than, to flowers, the dew-drop tear.
Thy wise instructive lessons please me well:
I'll go and practise them. Farewell, farewell!
    PRACTISE them. Farewell, farewell!

LESS AND MORE.

TWO prayers, dear Lord, in one—
  Give me both less and more;
Less of the impatient world, and more of Thee;
  Less of myself, and all that heretofore
Made me to slip where willing feet do run,
And held me back from where I fain would be—
  Kept me, my Lord, from Thee!

All things which most I need
  Are Thine; Thou wilt bestow
Both strength and shield, and be my willing Guest
  Yet my weak heart takes up a broken reed,
Thy rod and staff doth readily forego,
And I, who might be rich, am poor, distressed,
  And seek, but have not rest.

How long, O Lord, how long?
  So have I cried of late,
As though I knew not what I well do know:
  Come Thou, Great Master Builder, and create
Anew that which is Thine; undo my wrong—
Breathe on this waste, and life and health bestow
  Come, Lord, let it be so!

Let it be so, and then—
What then? My soul shall wait,
And ever pray—all prayers, dear Lord, in one—
Thy will o'er mine in all this mortal state
Hold regal sway. To Thy commands, Amen!
Break from my waiting lips till work is done,
   And crown and glory won.

COMFORT BY THE WAY.

I JOURNEY through a desert drear and wild,
   Yet is my heart by such sweet thoughts
      beguiled,
Of Him on whom I lean—my strength and stay—
I can forget the sorrows of the way.

Thoughts of His love! the root of every grace
Which finds in this poor heart a dwelling-place;
The sunshine of my soul, than day more bright,
And my calm pillow of repose by night.

Thoughts of His sojourn in this vale of tears,
The tale of love unfolded in those years

Of sinless suffering and patient grace
I love again, and yet again, to trace.

Thoughts of His glory! on the cross I gaze,
And there behold its sad, yet healing rays;
Beacon of hope! which, lifted up on high,
Illumes with heavenly light the tear-dimmed eye.

Thoughts of His coming! For that joyful day
In patient hope I watch, and wait, and pray;
The dawn draws nigh, the midnight shadows flee,
And what a sunrise will that advent be.

Thus while I journey on, my Lord to meet,
My thoughts and meditations are so sweet
Of Him on whom I lean—my strength, my stay
I can forget the sorrows of the way.

RETROSPECT.

O LOVING One! O Bounteous One!
    What have I not received from Thee
Throughout the seasons that have gone
    Into the past eternity!

Lowly my name and mine estate;
    Yet, Father, many a child of Thine,

Of purer heart and cleaner hands,
Walks in an humbler path than mine.

And, looking backward through the year
Along the way my feet have pressed,
I see sweet places everywhere—
Sweet places where my soul had rest.

For, though some human hopes of mine
Are dead, and buried from my sight,
Yet from their graves immortal flowers
Have sprung, and blossomed into light.

Body, and heart, and soul have been
Fed by the most convenient food;
My nights are peaceful all the while,
And all my mortal days are good.

My sorrows have not been so light
Thy chastening hand I could not trace;
Nor have my blessings been so great
That they have hid my Father's face.

HOW DOTH DEATH SPEAK OF OUR BELOVED?

> "The rain that falls upon the height,
> Too gently to be called delight,
> In the dark valley reappears
> As a wild cataract of tears:
> And love in life shall strive to see
> Sometimes what love in death would be."
> *Angel in the House.*

HOW doth Death speak of our beloved,
When it hath laid them low;
When it has set its hallowing touch
On speechless lip and brow?

It clothes their every gift and grace
With radiance from the holiest place,
With light as from an angel's face;

Recalling with resistless force
And tracing to their hidden source,
Deeds scarcely noticed in their course.

This little loving fond device,
That daily act of sacrifice,
Of which too late we learn the price!

Opening our weeping eyes to trace
Simple, unnoticed kindnesses,
Forgotten notes of tenderness,

Which evermore to us must be
Sacred as hymns in infancy,
Learned listening at a mother's knee.

Thus doth Death speak of our beloved
  When it has laid them low :
Then let Love antedate the work of Death,
  And do this now!

How doth Death speak of our beloved,
  When it has laid them low;
When it has set its hallowing touch
  On speechless lip and brow?

It sweeps their faults with heavy hand,
As sweeps the sea the trampled sand,
Till scarce the faintest print is scanned.

It shows how such a vexing deed
Was but generous nature's weed,
Or some choice virtue run to seed;

How that small fretting fretfulness
Was but love's over-anxiousness,
Which had not been, had love been less.

This failing, at which we repined,
But the dim shade of day declined,
Which should have made us doubly kind.

Thus doth Death speak of our beloved,
  When it has laid them low;
Then let Love antedate the work of Death
  And do this now!

———

How doth Death speak of our beloved,
  When it has laid them low;
When it has set its hallowing touch
  On speechless lip and brow?

It takes each failing on our part,
And brands it in upon the heart,
With caustic power and cruel art.

The small neglect that may have pained,
A giant stature will have gained
When it can never be explained:

The little service which had proved
How tenderly we watched and loved,
And those mute lips to glad smiles moved.

The little gift from out our store,
Which might have cheered some cheerless hour
When they with earth's poor needs were poor,
But never will be needed more!

It shows our faults like fires at night;
It sweeps their failings out of sight,
It clothes their good in heavenly light.

O Christ our life! fore-date the work of Death
   And do this now!
Thou art love, thus hallow our beloved!
   Not Death, but Thou!

A CHRISTMAS HYMN.

IN human form enthroned
   The sin of man atoned,
Immanuel sits in highest seat of heaven;
   Our nature there He wears,
   And that blest union bears,
In David's city on the low earth given.

   He draws us by a love,
   Not such as seraphs move
In happy life through all the realms of space;
   More subtle is the chord,
   The speaking of a word
In language learned among our fleshly race.

   "My blood, once flowing free
   Upon the darkened tree,

Gives life to you in heaven's eternal room;
  The brother and the friend,
  Through ages without end,
Shall e'en outlast the Saviour from the doom.'

THE WAY, THE TRUTH, AND THE LIFE.

THOU art the Way!
 All ways are thorny mazes without Thee;
Where hearts are pierced, and thoughts all aimless stray,
 In Thee the heart stands firm, the life moves free:
  Thou art our Way!

  Thou art the Truth;
Questions the ages break against in vain,
 Confront the spirit in its untried youth;
It starves while learning poison from the grain:
  Thou art the Truth!

  Thou art the Truth!
Truth for the mind, grand, glorious, infinite,
 A heaven still boundless o'er its highest growth
Bread for the heart its daily need to meet:
  Thou art the Truth!

Thou art the Light!
Earth beyond earth no faintest ray can give;
 Heaven's shadeless noontide blinds our mortal
  sight;
In Thee we look on God, and love and live:
 Thou art our Light!

Thou art the Rock!
Doubts none can solve heave wild on every side,
 Wave meeting wave of thought in ceaseless
  shock;
On Thee the soul rests calm amidst the tide:
 Thou art the Rock!

Thou art the Life!
All ways without Thee paths that end in death;
 All life without Thee with death's harvest rife
All truths dry bones, disjoined and void of breath
 Thou art our Life!

For Thou art Love!
Our Way and End! the way is rest with Thee!
 O living Truth! the truth is life in Thee!
O Life essential! life is bliss with Thee!
 For Thou art Love!

THE TIME FOR PRAYER.

WHEN is the time for prayer?
    With the first beams that light the morning sky;
Ere for the toils of day thou dost prepare,
    Lift up Thy thoughts on high;
Commend thy loved ones to His watchful care:
    Morn is the time for prayer.

And in the noontide hour,
    If worn by toil, or by sad cares oppressed,
Then unto God thy spirit's sorrow pour,
    And He will give thee rest;
Thy voice shall reach Him through the fields o'
    air:
Noon is the time for prayer.

When the bright sun hath set,
    While eve's bright colors deck the skies;
When with the loved at home again thou'st met
    Then let thy prayers arise;
For those who in thy joys and sorrows share
    Eve is the time for prayer.

And when the stars come forth—
    When to the trusting heart sweet hopes are given,

And the deep stillness of the hour gives birth
To pure bright dreams of heaven;
Kneel to thy God—ask strength, life's ills to bear
Night is the time for prayer.

When is the time for prayer?
In *every hour*, while life is spared to thee;
In crowds or solitude, in joy or care,
Thy thoughts should heavenward flee.
At home, at morn and eve, with loved ones there,
Bend thou the knee in prayer!

LIGHT IN DARKNESS.

BREEZES of spring, all earth to life awaking,
Birds swiftly soaring through the sunny sky,
The butterfly its lonely prison breaking,
The seed up-springing which had seemed to die.

Types such as these a word of hope have spoken,
Have shed a gleam of light around the tomb;
But weary hearts longed for a surer token,
A clearer ray, to dissipate its gloom.

And this was granted! See the Lord ascending
On crimson clouds of evening calmly borne.

With hands out-stretched, and looks of love still
    bending
On His bereaved ones, who no longer mourn.

I am the resurrection!" hear Him saying,
  "I am the life; he who believes in me
Shall never die; the souls my call obeying,
  Soon where I am for evermore shall be."

Sing hallelujah! light from heaven appearing,
  The mystery of life and death is plain;
Now to the grave we can descend unfearing,
  In sure and certain hope to rise again!

COMMUNION WITH GOD.

LORD, I am come along with Thee!
    Thy voice to hear, Thy face to see
      And feel Thy presence near;
It is not fancy's lovely dream,
Though wondrous e'en to faith it seem,
      That Thou dost wait me here.

A moment from this outward life,
Its service, self-denial, strife,
      I joyfully retreat;
My soul, through intercourse with Thee,

Strengthened, refreshed, and calmed shall be,
Its scenes again to meet.

How can it be that one so mean,
A sinner, selfish, dark, unclean,
    Thus in the Holiest stands?
And in that light divinely pure
Which may no stain of sin endure,
    Lifts up rejoicing hands!

Jesus! the answer Thou hast given!
Thy death, Thy life have opened heaven
    And all its joys to me;
Washed in Thy blood—oh! wondrous grace,
I'm holy as the Holy Place
    In which I worship Thee.

How sweet, how solemn thus to lie,
And feel Jehovah's searching eye
    On me well pleased can rest!
Because with His Beloved Son,
The Father's grace has made me *one*,
    I must be always blest.

The secret pangs I could not tell
To dearest friend—*Thou* knowest well;
    They claim Thy gracious heart:
Thou dost remove with tender care,

Or sweetly give me strength to bear
    The sanctifying smart.

Thy presence has a wondrous power!
The sharpest thorn becomes a flower,
        And breathes a sweet perfume;
Whate'er looked dark and sad before,
With happy light shines silvered o'er,
        There's no such thing as gloom

Thou know'st I have a cross to bear;
The needful stroke Thou dost not spare,
        To keep me near Thy side;
But when I see the chastening rod
In Thy pierced hand, my Lord, my God!
        I feel so satisfied!

Now, while I tell Thee how, within,
I oft indulge my bosom sin,
        How faithless oft I prove,
No cold repulse, no frown I meet,
But tender, soul-subduing, sweet
        Is the rebuke of Love.

THE SUFFERER CHEERED.

"SAY! shall I take the thorn away?"
   So spake my gracious Lord—
"O'er which thy sighs are heaved by day,
   Thy nightly tears are poured?
Say! shall I give thee rest and care,
   Make earth's fair prospects rise,
And bid thy bark o'er summer seas
   Float smoothly to the skies?

"Shall peace and plenty's cup swell high,
   Health leap through every vein,
And all exempt thy moments fly
   From bitter inward pain?
Be naught to check the inspiring flow
   Of human friendship's tide;
And every want thy heart can know,
   Be quickly satisfied?

"Know, thine ease-loving heart might miss
   The *comfort* with the *care!*
And that full tide of earthly bliss
   Leave little room for prayer!
Few were thy visits to the throne,
   Unhastened there by pain;
Thou, o'er thy bosom-sins, alone,
   Wouldst small advantage gain!

"Nor deem the highest, holiest joy
  A stranger still to woe;
Blest servants in my high employ,
  Most closely linked they go.
My love illumes with tenderest rays
  The path of self-denial;
And burning bright the glory's blaze
  That crowns the fiery trial!

"In conscious weakness thou shalt hang
  On my almighty arm!
Soon as the thorn inflicts its pang,
  I'll pour my love's rich balm.
Thou plainest in thy deepest woe
  Shall feel me at thy side;
And, for my praise, to all shalt show,
  Thou art well satisfied.

'Then, wilt thou in thy Master's cup
  Consent awhile to share?
Know, when in love I drank it up,
  No *wrath* was left thee there!
Thy Saviour's love and power to bless,
  Trust where thou canst not *see!*
And in yon howling wilderness
  Step fearless forth with me!"

"Lord! magnify Thyself in me!"
  With faltering lips I said;
For, strong to bear as faith may be,
  Weak nature quails with dread;
But He who through the shrinking flesh
  The spirit's will can read,
Smiled on His work, and bade afresh
  ALL GRACE MEET ALL MY NEED.

ALL IN CHRIST.

IN Thee my heart, O Jesus! finds repose;
  Thou bringest rest to all that weary are;
Until that Day-spring from on high arose,
  I wandered through a night without a star;
    My feet had gone astray
    Upon a lonely way:
Each guide I followed failed me in my need;
Each staff I leaned on proved a broken reed.

Then, when in mine extremity to Thee
  turned, Thy pity did prevent my prayer,
From that entangling maze it set me free,
  And quickly loosed my heavy load of care,

Gave me the lofty scope
Of a heaven-centred hope,
And led me on with Thee, a gentle Guide,
Thither, where pure immortal joys abide.

Thou art the great completion of my soul,
　The blest fulfillment of its deepest need;
When self-surrendered to Thy mild control,
　It enters into liberty indeed;
　　Thy love a genial law,
　　Its very aim doth draw
Within its holy range, and sweetly lure
　Its longings toward the beautiful and pure.

Thy presence is the never-failing spring
　Of life and comfort in each darker hour;
And through Thy grace, benignly ministering,
　Grief wields a secret, purifying power.
　　'Tis sweet, O Lord! to know
　　Thy kindredness with woe;
Sweeter to walk with Thee on ways apart
Than with the world, where heart is shut to heart!

For Thee eternity reserves her hymn;
　For Thee earth has her prayers and heaven her
　　　　vows;
Thy saints adore Thee, and the seraphim,
　Under Thy glory, stoop their starry brows.

Oh! may that light divine
On me still clearer shine—
A power, an inspiration from above,
Lifting me higher to Thy perfect love!

"HIMSELF HATH DONE IT."

"HIMSELF hath done it" all! Oh how those words
Should hush to silence every murmuring thought—
Himself hath done it—He who loves me best,
He who my soul with His own blood hath bought.

"Himself hath done it!" Can it then be aught
Than full of wisdom, full of tenderest love?
Not *one* unneeded sorrow will He send,
To teach this wandering heart no more to rove.

"Himself hath done it!" Yes, although severe
May seem the stroke, and bitter be the cup,
'Tis His own hand that holds it, and I know
He'll give me grace to drink it meekly up.

"Himself hath done it!" Oh! no arm but His
Could e'er sustain beneath earth's dreary lot;
But while I know He's doing all things well,
My heart His loving-kindness questions not.

"Himself hath done it!" He who's searched me
    through,
Sees how I cleave to earth's ensnaring ties;
And so He breaks each reed on which my soul
    Too much for happiness and joy relies.

"Himself hath done it!" He would have me see
    What broken cisterns human friends *must* prove:
That I may turn and quench my burning thirst
    At His own fount of *ever-living* love.

"Himself hath done it!" Then I fain would say,
    "Thy will in *all* things evermore be done;"
E'en though that will remove whom best I love,
    While Jesus lives I can not be alone.

"Himself hath done it!" Precious, precious
    words,
"Himself," my Father, Saviour, Brother, Friend;
Whose faithfulness no variation knows;
    Who, having loved me, loves me *to the end*.

And when in His eternal presence blest,
    I at His feet my crown immortal cast,
I'll gladly own, with all His ransomed saints,
    "Himself hath done it"—all, from first to last!

LIVING WATERS.

IN some wild Eastern legend the story has been told,
Of a fair and wondrous fountain that flowed in times of old;
Cold and crystalline its waters, brightly glancing in the ray
Of the summer moon at midnight, or the sun at height of day.

And a good angel, resting there, once in a favored hour,
Infused into the limpid depths a strange mysterious power:
A hidden principle of life, to rise and gush again,
Where but some drops were scattered on the dry and barren plain.

So the traveler might journey, not now in fear and haste,
Far through the mountain-desert, far o'er the sandy waste,

If but he sought this fountain first, and from its
 wondrous store
The secret of unfailing springs along with him he
 bore.

Wild and fanciful the legend—yet may not mean-
 ings high,
Visions of better things to come, within its shadow
 lie?
Type of a better fountain, to mortals now un-
 sealed.
The full and free salvation in Christ our Lord re-
 vealed?

Beneath the Cross those waters rise, and he who
 finds them there
All through the wilderness of life the living stream
 may bear;
And blessings follow in his steps, until where'er
 he goes,
The moral wastes begin to bud and blossom as
 the rose.

Ho! every one that thirsteth, come to this fount-
 ain side!
Drink freely of its waters, drink, and be satisfied

Yet linger not, but hasten on, and bear to all
    around
Glad tidings of the love and peace, and mercy
    thou hast found!

To Afric's pathless deserts, to Greenland's frozen
    shore—
Where din of mighty cities sounds, or savage
    monsters roar—
Wherever man may wander with his heritage of
    woe,
To tell of brighter things above, go, brothers,
    gladly go!

Then, as of old in vision seen before the prophet's
    eyes,
Broader and deeper on its course the stream of
    life shall rise;
And everywhere, as on it flows, shall carry light
    and love,
Peace and good-will to man on earth, glory to
    God above!

ABIDE WITH US.

THE tender light is fading where
   We pause and linger still,
And, through the dim and saddened air,
   We feel the evening chill.

Long hast Thou journeyed with us, Lord
   Ere we Thy face did know;
Oh! still Thy fellowship afford,
   While dark the shadows grow.

For passed is many a beauteous field,
   Beside our morning road;
And many a fount to us is sealed
   That once so freshly flowed.

The splendor of the noontide lies
   On other paths than ours;
The dews that lave yon fragrant skies
   Will not revive our flowers.

It is not now as in the glow
   Of life's impassioned heat,
When to the heart there seemed to flow
   All that of earth was sweet.

Something has faded—something died—
Without us and within;
We more than ever need a guide;
Blinded and weak with sin.

The weight is heavy that we bear,
  Our strength more feeble grows!
Weary with toil and pain and care,
  We long for sweet repose.

Stay with us, gracious Saviour, stay
  While friends and hopes depart!
Fainting, on Thee we wish to lay
  The burden of our heart.

Abide with us, dear Lord! remain
  Our Life, our Truth, our Way!
So shall our loss be turned to gain—
  Night drawn to endless day,

THE BETTER LIFE.

"ALL the way by which the Lord thy God led thee."

WHEN we reach a quiet dwelling
   On the strong eternal hills,
And our praise to Him is swelling,
   Who the vast creation fills:
When the paths of prayer and duty
   And affliction all are trod,
And we wake and see the beauty
   Of our Saviour and our God;

With the light of resurrection,
   When our changèd bodies glow,
And we gain the full perfection
   Of the bliss begun below:
When the life that flesh obscureth
   In each radiant form shall shine,
And the joy that aye endureth
   Flashes forth in beams divine.

While we wave the palms of glory
   Through the long eternal years,
Shall we e'er forget the story
   Of our mortal griefs and fears?

Shall we e'er forget the sadness
  And the clouds that hung so dim,
When our hearts are filled with gladness
  And our tears are dried by Him?

Shall the memory be banished
  Of His kindness and His care,
When the wants and woes are vanished,
  Which He loved to soothe and share—
All the way by which He brought us,
  All the grievings which He bore,
All the patient love He taught us,
  Shall we think of them no more?

Yes! we surely shall remember
  How He quickened us from death:
How He fanned the dying ember
  With His Spirit's glowing breath.
We shall read the tender meaning
  Of the sorrows and alarms
As we trod the desert, leaning
  On His everlasting arms.

And His rest will be the dearer
  When we think of weary ways,
And His light will seem the clearer
  As we muse on cloudy days.

Oh! 'twill be a glorious morrow
To a dark and stormy day;
We shall recollect our sorrow
As the streams that pass away.

PRAY FOR WHOM THOU LOVEST.

Pray for whom thou lovest; thou wilt never have any comfort of his friendship for whom thou dost not pray.

YES, pray for whom thou lovest; thou may'st
vainly, idly seek
The fervid words of tenderness by feeble words
to speak;
Go kneel before thy Father's throne, and meekly,
humbly there
Ask blessing for the loved one in the silent hour
of prayer.

Yes, pray for whom thou lovest; if uncounted
wealth were thine—
The treasures of the boundless deep, the riches
of the mine—
Thou could'st not to thy cherished friends a gift
so dear impart,
As the earnest benediction of a deeply-loving
heart.

Seek not the worldling's friendship, it shall droop
    and wave ere long
In the cold and heartless glitter of the pleasure
    loving throng;
But seek the friend who when thy prayer for him
    shall murmured be,
Breathes forth in faithful sympathy a fervent
    prayer for thee.

And should thy flowery path of life become a
    path of pain,
The friendship formed in bonds like these thy
    spirit shall sustain,
Years may not chill, nor change invade, nor poverty impair,
The love that grew and flourished at the holy
    time of prayer.

DRAWING WATER.

I HAD drank with lip unsated
    Where the founts of pleasure burst;
I had hewn out broken cisterns,
    And they mocked my spirit's thirst.

And I said, Life is a desert,
    Hot and measureless and dry;

And God will not give me water,
   Though I pray and faint and die!

Spoke there then a friend and brother,
   "Rise and roll the stone away!
There are founts of life upspringing
   In thy pathway every day."

Then I said my heart was sinful—
   Very sinful was my speech;
All the wells of God's salvation
   Are too deep for me to reach.

And he answered: "Rise and labor!
   Doubt and idleness is death;
Shape thou out a goodly vessel
   With the strong hands of thy faith."

So I wrought and shaped the vessel,
   Then knelt lowly, humbly there;
And I drew up living water
   With the golden chain of prayer.

A TRUE DREAM.

I DREAMT we danced in careless glee,
With hearts and footsteps light and free,
That one so dearly loved and I,
As in the childish days gone by
   Forever.

I felt her arms around me fold,
I heard her soft laugh as of old ;
Her eyes with smiles were brimming o'er—
Eyes we may meet on earth no more
   Forever.

Then there came mingling with my dreams
 A sense perplexed of loss and change—
  An echo dim of time and tears;
Until I said : "How long it seems
 Since thus we danced ! Is it not strange?
  Do you not feel the weight of years?
Or dread life's evening shadows cold?
Or mourn to think we must grow old?"
Wondering, she paused a little while,
Then answered, with a radiant smile:
   "No, never!"

Wondering as if to her I told
    The customs of some foreign land,
Or spoke a tongue she knew of old,
    But could no longer understand;
Till o'er her face that sunshine broke,
And with that radiant smile she spoke
              That "Never.'

But not until the dream had fled
I knew the sense of what she said;
Young with immortal truth and love,
Child in the Father's house above
              Forever.

We echo back thy words again;
They smite us with no grief or pain;
We journey not toward the night,
But to the breaking of the light
              Together.

Our life is no poor cisterned store,
    The lavish years are draining low;
But living streams that, welling o'er,
    Fresh from the Living Fountain flow
              Forever.

"O LORD! THOU KNOWEST."

THOU knowest, Lord, the weariness and sor-
row
Of the sad heart that comes to Thee for rest,
Cares of to-day, and burdens for to-morrow,
Blessings implored, and sins to be confessed;
I come before Thee at Thy gracious word,
And lay them at Thy feet—Thou knowest, Lord.

Thou knowest all the past; how long and blindly
    On the dark mountains the lost wanderer strayed;
How the good Shepherd followed, and how kindly
    He bore it home, upon His shoulders laid;
And healed the bleeding wounds, and soothed the pain,
And brought back life, and hope, and strength again.

Thou knowest all the present, each temptation,
    Each toilsome duty, each foreboding fear;
All to myself assigned of tribulation,
    Or to belovèd ones, than self more dear!
All pensive memories, as I journey on,
Longings for vanished smiles, and voices gone!

Thou knowest all the future: gleams of gladness
   By stormy clouds too quickly overcast;
Hours of sweet fellowship, and parting sadness,
   And the dark river to be crossed at last:
Oh! what could confidence and hope afford
To tread that path, but this—*thou knowest, Lord!*

Thou knowest, not alone as God, all-knowing;
   As man, our mortal weakness Thou hast proved;
On earth, with purest sympathies o'erflowing,
   O Saviour! Thou hast wept, and Thou hast loved!
And Love and Sorrow still to Thee may come,
And find a hiding-place, a rest, a home.

Therefore I come, Thy gentle call obeying,
   And lay my sins and sorrows at Thy feet;
On everlasting strength my weakness staying,
   Clothed in Thy robe of righteousness complete
Then rising and refreshed, I leave Thy throne,
And follow on to know as I am known!

MINISTRY.

"THE Son of Man came not to be ministered unto, but to minister."

SINCE service is the highest lot,
    And all are in one Body bound,
In all the world the place is not
    Which may not with this bliss be crowned

The sufferer on the bed of pain
    Need not be laid aside from this;
But for each kindness gives again
    "This joy of doing kindnesses."

The poorest may enrich this feast,
    Not one lives only to receive;
But renders through the hands of Christ
    Richer returns than man can give.

The little child, in trustful glee,
    With love and gladness brimming o'er,
Many a cup of ministry
    May for the weary veteran pour.

The lonely glory of a throne
    May yet this lowly joy preserve;

Love may make that a stepping-stone,
    And raise " I reign " into " I serve."

This, by the ministries of prayer,
    The loneliest life with blessings crowds;
Can consecrate each petty care,
    Make angels' ladders out of clouds.

Nor serve we only when we gird
    Our hearts for special ministry;
That creature best has ministered
    Which is what it was meant to be.

Birds, by being glad, their Maker bless;
    By simply shining, sun and star;
And we, whose law is love, serve less
    By what we do than what we are.

Since service is the highest lot,
    And angels know no higher bliss,
Then with what good her cup is fraught
    Who was created but for this!

IT IS WELL.

SO they said, who saw the wonders
   Of Messiah's power and love;
So they sing, who see His glory
   In the Father's house above;
Ever reading, in each record
   Of the strangely varied past,
" All was well which God appointed,
   All has wrought for good at last."

And on earth we hear the echoes
   Of that chorus in the sky;
Through the day of toil or weeping,
   Faith can raise a glad reply.
It is well, O saints departed!
   Well with you, forever blest.
Well with us, who journey forward
   To your glory and your rest!

Times are changing, days are flying,
   Years are quickly past and gone,
While the wildly mingled murmur
   Of life's busy hum goes on;
Sounds of tumult, sounds of triumph,
   Marriage chimes and passing-bell;
Yet through all one key-note sounding,
   Angels' watchword: " It is well,"

We may hear it, through the rushing
   Of the midnight tempest's wave;
We may hear it, through the weeping
   Round the newly covered grave;
In the dreary house of mourning,
   In the darkened room of pain,
If we listen meekly, rightly,
   We may catch that soothing strain.

For Thine arm Thou hast not shortened,
   Neither turned away Thine ear,
O Saviour! ever ready
   The afflicted's prayer to hear!
Show us light, still surely resting
   Over all Thy darkest ways;
Give us faith, still surely trusting
   Through the sad and evil days.

And thus, while years are fleeting,
   Though our joys are with them gone,
In Thy changeless love rejoicing
   We shall journey calmly on;
Till at last, all sorrow over,
   Each our tale of grace shall tell,
In the heavenly chorus joining:
   "Lord, Thou hast done all things well!"

I.

THE CROSS.

"Now there stood by the Cross of Jesus, His mother."

THE strongest light casts deepest shade,
　The dearest love makes dreariest loss,
And she His birth so blessed had made,
　Stood by Him dying on the cross.

Yet since not grief but joy shall last,
　The day and not the night abide,
And all time's shadows, earthward cast,
　Are lights upon the "other side;"

Through what long bliss that shall not fail,
　That darkest hour shall brighten on!
Better than any angel's "*Hail!*"
　The memory of "*Behold thy Son!*"

Blessed in thy lowly heart to store
　The homage paid at Bethlehem;
But far more blessed evermore,
　Thus to have shared the taunts and shame.

Thus with thy pierced heart to have stood
　'Mid mocking crowds and owned Him thine
True through a world's ingratitude,
　And owned in death by lips Divine.

II.

THE CROWN.

THOU shalt be crowned, O mother blest!
    Our hearts behold thee crowned e'en now
The crown of motherhood, earth's best,
    O'ershadowing thy maiden brow.

Thou shalt be crowned! More fragrant bays
    Than ever poet's brows entwine,
For thine immortal hymn of praise,
    First Singer of the Church, are thine.

Thou shalt be crowned! all earth and heaven
    Thy coronation pomp shall see;
The Hand by which thy crown is given,
    Shall be no stranger's hand to thee.

Thou shalt be crowned! but not a queen;
    A better triumph ends thy strife:
Heaven's bridal raiment, white and clean,
    The victor's crown of fadeless life.

Thou shalt be crowned! but not alone—
    No lonely pomp shall weigh thee down;
Crowned with the myriads round His throne,
    And casting at His feet thy crown.

PRAYER OUT OF THE DEPTHS.

ALL in weakness, all in sorrow,
   O my God! I come once more,
Lifting up the sad petition
   Thou hast often heard before—
In the former days of darkness,
   In the time of need of yore.

For a present help in trouble
   Thou hast never ceased to be;
Since at first a weeping sinner
   Fell before Thee trustingly;
And Thy voice is ever sounding:
   "O ye weary! come to Me."

Lord, Thou knowest all the weakness
   Of the creatures Thou hast made,
For with mortal imperfection
   Thou didst once Thy glory shade;
Thou hast loved and Thou hast sorrowed
   In the veil of flesh arrayed.

Thus I fear not to approach Thee
   With my sorrow and my care;
Hear my mourning supplication,
   Cast not out my humble prayer!

Lay not on a greater burden
   Than Thy feeble child can bear!

Earth has lost its best attractions,
   All the brightest stars are gone—
All is clouded now and cheerless,
   Where so long a glory shone:
Where I walked with loved companions,
   I must wander now alone.

All is dark on the horizon,
   Clouds returning after rain;
Faith is languid, Hope is weary,
   And the questions rise again:
'Doth the promise fail forever?
   Hast Thou made all men in vain?

O my God! rebuke the tempter,
   Let not unbelief prevail!
Pray for me, Thy feeble servant,
   That my weak faith may not fail,
Nor my Hope let go her anchor
   When the waves and storms assail!

All these passing changing shadows,
   All these brief, bright joys below—
Let me grasp them not so closely,
   Nor desire nor prize them so!

Nor endure this bitter anguish,
  When Thou bid'st me let them go!

O Redeemer! shall one perish
  Who has looked to Thee for aid?
Let me see Thee, let me hear Thee,
  Through the gloomy midnight shade;
Let me hear Thy voice of comfort:
  " It is I, be not afraid!"

For when feeling *Thou* art near me,
  All my loneliness is o'er,
And the tempter's dark suggestions
  Can oppress my soul no more;
I shall dread the path no longer
  Where Thyself hast gone before.

And the lights of earth all fading,
  I can gaze on tearlessly,
When the glory that excelleth,
  When the light of life I see:
Whom besides, in earth or heaven,
  Should my heart desire, but Thee?

SALOME.

SHE knew not what for them she sought
   At His right hand and left to sit!
How great the glory, passing thought;
   How rough the path that led to it.

They knew not what of Him they asked;
   But He their deeper sense distilled;
Gently the selfish wish unmasked,
   But all the prayer of love fulfilled.

Pride sought to lift herself on high,
   And heard but of the bitter cup;
Love would but to her Lord be nigh,
   And won her measure full—heaped up

With vision of His glory blessed;
   Stood on the mountain by His side;
Leaned, at the Supper, on His breast;
   Stood close beneath Him when He died

One brother shared His cup of woe—
   The second of His martyr-band;
One, by His glory smitten low,
   Rose at the touch of His right hand.

Thus, when by earth's cross lights perplexed,
We crave the thing that should not be,
God reading right our erring text,
Gives what we would ask, could we see.

MEMORIES.

WHEN fall the evening shadows, long and
deep, across the hill ;
When all the air is fragrance, and all the breezes
still ;

When the summer sun seems pausing above the
mountain's brow,
As if he left reluctantly a scene so lovely now ;

Then I linger on the pathway, and I fondly gaze,
and long,
As if reading some old story those deep purple
clouds among ;

Then Memory approaches, holding up her magic
glass,
Pointing to familiar figures, which across the surface pass.

And often do I question, as I view that phantom train,
Whether most with joy or sadness I behold them thus again.

They are there, those scenes of beauty, when life's brightest hours have fled,
And I haste, with dear companions, the old paths again to tread;

But, suddenly dissolving, all the loveliness is flown,
And I find a thorny wilderness, where I must walk alone.

Thou art there so loved and honored, as in each former hour :
When we read thine eye's deep meaning, when we heard thy words of power;

When our souls as willing captives, have sought to follow thine,
Tracing the eternal footsteps of Might and Love Divine.

But o'er that cherished image falls a veil of clouds and gloom,
And beside a bier I tremble, or I weep above a tomb.

And ever will the question come, O Memory!
  again,
Whether in thy magic mirror there is most of
  bliss or pain?

Would I not wish the brightness were forever hid
  from view,
If but those hours of darkness could be all for-
  gotten too?

Then, weary and desponding, my spirit seeks to
  rise
Away from earthly conflicts, from mortal smiles
  or sighs.

I do not think the blessèd ones with Jesus have
  forgot
The changing joys and sorrows which have marked
  their earthly lot;

But now, on Memory's record their eyes can
  calmly dwell;
They can see, what here they trusted—God hath
  done all things well;

And vain regrets and longings are as old things
  passed away;
No shadows dim the sunshine of that bright eter-
  nal day!

THE WIDOW OF NAIN.

THY miracles are no state splendors
  Whose pomps Thy daily works excel;
The rock which breaks the stream, but renders
  Its constant current audible.

The power which startles us in thunders
  Works ever silently in light ·
And mightier than these special wonders
  The wonders daily in our sight.

Rents in the veils Thy works that fold,
  They let the inner light shine through;
The rent is new, the light is old,
  Eternal, never ever new.

And, therefore, when Thy touch arrests
  The bearers of that bier at Nain,
Warm on unnumbered hearts it rests,
  Though yet their dead live not again.

And Thy compassionate "Weep not!"
  On this our tearful earth once heard,
For every age with comfort fraught,
  Tells how Thy heart is ever stirred.

Nature repeats the tale each year,
  She feels Thy touch through countless springs
And, rising from her wintry bier,
  Throws off her grave-clothes, lives, and sings.

And when Thy touch through earth shall thrill
  This bier whereon our race is laid,
And, for the first time standing still,
  The long procession of the dead

At Thy "Arise!" shall wake from clay,
  Young, deathless, freed from every stain;
When Thy "Weep not!" shall wipe away
  Tears that shall never come again;

When the strong chains of death are burst,
  And lips long dumb begin to speak,
What name will each then utter first?
  What music shall that silence break?

PATHWAYS OF THE HOLY LAND.

THE pathways of Thy land are little changed
    Since Thou wert there:
The busy world through other ways has ranged,
    And left these bare.

The rocky path still climbs the glowing steep
    Of Olivet,
Though rains of two millenniums wear it deep.
    Men tread it yet.

Still to the gardens o'er the brook it leads,
    Quiet and low:
Before his sheep the shepherd on it treads,
    His voice they know.

The wild fig throws broad shadows o'er it still,
    As once o'er Thee;
Peasants go home at evening up that hill
    To Bethany.

And, as when gazing Thou didst weep o'er them
    From height to height
The white roofs of discrowned Jerusalem
    Burst on our sight.

These ways were strewed with garments once, and
 palm,
 Which we tread thus ;
Here, through Thy triumph, on Thou passedst,
 calm,
 On to Thy cross.

The waves have washed fresh sands upon the shore
 Of Galilee ;
But, chiseled in the hillsides, evermore
 Thy paths we see.

Man has not changed them in that slumbering
 land,
 Nor time effaced ;
Where Thy feet trod to bless, we still may stand,
 All can be traced.

Yet we have traces of Thy footsteps far
 Truer than these ;
Where'er the poor, and tried, and suffering are,
 Thy steps faith sees.

Nor with fond sad regrets Thy steps we trace ;
 Thou art not dead !

Our path is onward, till we see Thy face,
    And hear Thy tread.

And now, wherever meets Thy lowliest band
    In praise and prayer,
There is Thy presence, there Thy Holy Land,
    Thou, Thou art there!

FOR THE NEW YEAR.

ANOTHER year! another year!
    Has borne its record to the skies.
Another year! another year,
    Untried, unproved, before us lies;
We hail with smiles its dawning ray—
How shall we meet its final day?

Another year, another year!
    Its squandered hours will ne'er return.
Oh! many a heart must quail with fear
    O'er memory's blotted page to turn.
No record from that leaf will fade,
Not one erasure may be made.

Another year, another year!
How many a grief has marked its flight!
Some whom we love, no more are here—
Translated to the realms of light.
Ah! none can bless the coming year
Like those no more to greet us here.

Another year, another year!
Oh! many a blessing, too, was given,
Our lives to deck, our hearts to cheer,
And antedate the joys of heaven;
But they, too, slumber in the past,
Where joys and griefs must sink at last.

Another year, another year!
Gaze we no longer on the past.
Nor let us shrink, with faithless fear,
From the dark shade the future casts.
The past, the future—what are they
To those whose lives may end to-day?

Another year, another year!
Perchance the last of life below.
Who, ere its close, Death's call may hear:
None but the Lord of life can know.
Oh! to be found, whene'er that day
May come, prepared to pass away.

Another year, another year!
  Help us earth's thorny path to tread;
So may each moment bring us near
  To Thee, ere yet our lives are fled.
Saviour! we yield ourselves to Thee,
For time and for eternity.

THE PERPETUITY OF JOY IN HEAVEN

HERE brief is the sighing,
  And brief is the crying,
For brief is the life!
The life there is endless,
The joy there is endless,
  And ended the strife.

What joys are in heaven?
To whom are they given?
  Ah! what? and to whom?
The stars to the earth-born,
"Best robes" to the sin-worn,
  The crown for the doom!

O country the fairest!
Our country the dearest,

We press toward thee!
O Sion the golden!
Our eyes now are holden,
 Thy light till we see:

Thy crystalline ocean,
Unvexed by commotion,
 Thy fountain of life;
Thy deep peace unspoken,
Pure, sinless, unbroken—
 Thy peace beyond strife:

Thy meek saints all glorious,
Thy martyrs victorious,
 Who suffer no more;
Thy halls full of singing,
Thy hymns ever ringing
 Along Thy safe shore.

Like the lily for whiteness,
Like the jewel for brightness,
 Thy vestments, O Bride!
The Lamb ever with thee,
The Bridegroom is with thee—
 With thee to abide!

We know not, we know not,
All human words show not,

The joys we may reach;
The mansions preparing,
The joys for our sharing,
The welcome for each.

O Sion the golden!
My eyes still are holden,
Thy light till I see;
And deep in thy glory,
Unveiled then before me,
My King, look on thee.

THROUGH THE FLOOD ON FOOT.

THE sun had sunk in the West,
For a little while,
And the clouds which gathered to see him die
Had caught his dying smile.

We sat in the door of our Tent,
In the cool of the day,
Toward the quiet meadow
Where misty shadows lay.

The great and terrible Land
Of wilderness and drought,

Lay in the shadows behind us,
   For the Lord had brought us out.

The great and terrible River,
   Though shrouded still from view,
Lay in the shadows before us,
   But the Lord would bear us through.

In the stillness and the starlight,
   In sight of the Blessed Land,
We thought of the bygone Desert-life,
   And the burning, blinding sand.

Many a dreary sunset,
   Many a dreary dawn,
We had watched upon those desert hills
   As we pressed slowly on.

Yet sweet had been the silent dews
   Which from God's presence fell,
And the still hours of resting
   By Palm-tree and by Well;

Till we pitched our Tent at last
   The Desert done,
Where we saw the hills of the Holy Land
   Gleam in our sinking sun.

And we sat in the door of our Tent,
  In the cool of the day,
Toward the quiet meadow
  Where misty shadows lay :

We were talking about the King,
  And our elder Brother,
As we were used often to speak
  One to another.

The Lord standing quietly by,
  In the shadows dim,
Smiling perhaps, in the dark, to hear
  Our sweet, sweet talk of Him.

"I think in a little while,"
  I said at length,
"We shall see His face in the city
  Of everlasting strength ;

"And sit down under the shadow
  Of His smile,
With great delight and thanksgiving,
  To rest awhile."

"But the River—the awful River!
  In the dying light,"

And even as he spoke, the murmur
　Of a river rose on the night!

And One came up through the meadow,
　Where the mists lay dim,
Till He stood by my friend in the star-light,
　And spake to him :

" I have come to call thee Home,"
　Said our veilèd Guest ;
" The terrible journey of life is done,
　I will take thee into Rest.

" Arise ! thou shalt come to the Palace,
　To rest thee forever ; "
And He pointed across the dark meadow,
　And down to the River.

And my friend rose up in the shadows,
　And turned to me—
" Be of good cheer," I said faintly,
　" For He calleth thee."

For I knew by His loving voice,
　His kingly word,
The veilèd Guest in the star-light dim
　Was Christ, the Lord !

So we three went slowly down
  To the River-side,
Till we stood in the heavy shadows
  By the black, wild tide.

I could hear that the Lord was speaking
  Deep words of grace,
I could see their blessed reflection
  On my friend's pale face.

The strong and desolate tide
  Was hurrying wildly past,
As he turned to take my hand once more,
  And say Farewell, at last.

"Farewell—I can not fear,
  Oh! seest *thou* His grace?"
And even as he spoke, he turned
  Again to the Master's Face.

So they two went closer down
  To the River-side,
And stood in the heavy shadows
  By the black, wild tide.

But when the feet of the Lord
  Were come to the waters dim,
They rose to stand, on either hand,
  And left a path for Him;

So they two passed over swiftly
  Toward the Goal,
But the wistful, longing gaze
  Of the passing soul

Grew only more rapt and joyful
  As he clasped the Master's hand;
I think, or ever he was aware
  They were come to the Holy Land.

Now I sit alone in the door of my Tent
  In the cool of the day,
Toward the quiet meadow
  Where misty shadows play.

The great and terrible Land
  Of wilderness and drought,
Lies in the shadows behind me,
  For the Lord hath brought me out;

The great and terrible River,
  I stood that night to view,
Lies in the shadows before me,
  But the Lord will bear me through.

THE LONG GOOD-NIGHT.

I JOURNEY forth rejoicing,
    From this dark vale of tears,
To heavenly joy and freedom,
    From earthly bonds and fears;
Where Christ our Lord shall gather
    All His redeemed again,
His kingdom to inherit.
                Good-night, till then!

Go to thy quiet resting,
    Poor tenement of clay!
From all thy pain and weakness
    I gladly haste away;
But still in faith confiding
    To find thee yet again,
All glorious and immortal.
                Good-night, till then!

Why thus so sadly weeping,
    Beloved ones of my heart?
The Lord is good and gracious,
    Though now He bids us part.

Oft have we met in gladness,
  And we shall meet again,
All sorrow left behind us.
      Good-night, till then!

I go to see His glory,
  Whom we have loved below:
I go, the blessed angels,
  The holy saints to know.
Our lovely ones departed,
  I go to find again,
And wait for you to join us.
      Good-night, till then!

I hear the Saviour calling—
  The joyful hour has come:
The angel guards are ready
  To guide me to our home,
Where Christ our Lord shall gather
  All His redeemed again,
His kingdom to inherit.
      Good-night, till then!

FOOTSTEPS ON THE OTHER SIDE.

SITTING in my humble doorway,
   Gazing out into the night,
Listening to the stormy tumult
   With a kind of sad delight—
Wait I for the loved who comes not,
   One whose step I long to hear;
One who, though he lingers from me,
   Still is dearest of the dear.
Soft! he comes—now heart, be quick—
   Leaping in triumphant pride!
Oh! it is a stranger footstep,
   Gone by on the other side.

All the night seems filled with weeping;
   Winds are wailing mournfully;
And the rain-tears together
   Journey to the restless sea.
I can fancy, sea, your murmur,
   As they with your waters flow,
Like the griefs of single beings,
   Making up a nation's woe!

Branches, bid your guests be silent;
   Hush a moment, fretful rain;
Breeze, stop sighing—let me listen,
   God grant not again in vain!

In my cheek the blood is rosy,
  Like the blushes of a bride.
Joy! Alas! a stranger footstep
  Goes by on the other side.

Ah! how many wait forever
  For the steps that do not come!
Wait until the pitying angels
  Bear them to a peaceful home!
Many in the still of midnight
  In the streets have lain and died,
While the sound of human footsteps
  Went by on the other side.

GONE HOME.

GONE home! Gone home! She lingers here
    no longer
A restless pilgrim, walking painfully,
With home-sick longing, daily growing stronger,
  And yearning visions of the joys to be.

Gone home! Gone home! Her earnest, active
    spirit,
  Her very playfulness, her heart of love!
The heavenly mansion now she doth inherit,
  Which Christ made ready ere she went above.

Gone home! Gone home! The door through
    which she vanished
Closed with a jar, and left us here alone;
We stand without, in tears, forlorn and banished,
    Longing to follow where one loved has gone.

Gone home! Gone home! Oh! shall we ever
    reach her,
See her again, and know her for our own?
Will she conduct us to the heavenly Teacher,
    And bow beside us, low before His throne?

Gone home! Gone home! O human-hearted
    Saviour!
Give us a balm to soothe our heavy woe;
And if Thou wilt, in tender, pitying favor,
    Hasten the time when we may rise and go!

FUNERAL HYMN.

COME forth! come on, with solemn song
    The road is short, the rest is long;
The Lord brought here, He calls away;
    Make no delay,
This home was for a passing day.

Here in an inn a stranger dwelt,
Here joy and grief by turns he felt;
Poor dwelling, now we close thy door!
    Thy task is o'er,
The sojourner returns no more.

Now of a lasting home possessed,
He goes to seek a deeper rest.
Good-night! the day was sultry here
    In toil and fear;
Good-night! the night is cool and clear.

Chime on, ye bells! again begin,
And ring the Sabbath morning in;
The laborer's week-day work is done;
    The rest begun,
Which Christ hath for His people won.

Now open to us the gates of peace!
Here let the pilgrim's journey cease;
Ye quiet slumberers, make room
    In your still home
For the new stranger who has come!

How many graves around us lie!
How many homes are in the sky!

Yes, for each saint doth Christ prepare
   A place with care;
Thy home is waiting, brother, there.

Jesus, Thou reignest, Lord, alone;
Thou wilt return and claim Thine own;
Come quickly, Lord! return again!
   Amen! Amen!
Thine seal us ever, now and then.

WE ARE THE LORD'S.

WE are the Lord's. His, earthly life and
   spirit!
We are the Lord's, who once for all men died!
We are the Lord's, and shall all things inherit!
We are the Lord's, who wins us all beside!

We are the Lord's! So in most holy living,
   Glad let us, body, soul, be His alone;
And heart and mouth, and act join, witness giving
   That it is surely true: we are His own!

We are the Lord's! So in the dark vale gleaming
   One star dispels our fear, and keeping ward,

Doth light our way with sweet unchangeful beam-
    ing :
It is the precious Word. We're thine, O Lord

We are the Lord's! So will He on the morrow
  Watch our last pang, when other help rewards,
No pain, and Death brings not a touch of sorrow:
  This Word's forever true ; we are the Lord's.

EUTHANASY.

WE need no change of sphere
    To view the heavenly sights, or hear
The songs which angels sing. The hand
  Which gently pressed the sightless orbs ere-
    while,
  Giving them light, a world of beauty, and the
    friendly smile,
Can cause our eyes to see the better land.

  We need no wings
  To soar aloft to realms of higher things ;
But only feet which walk the paths of peace,
  Guided by Him whose voice
  Greets every ear, makes every heart rejoice,
Saying: Arise, and walk where sorrows cease.

Visiting spirits are near;
They are not wholly silent, but we can not hear
Nor understand their speech.
Our Saviour caught His Father's word,
And men of old, dreaming and walking, heard
The breathings of a world we can not reach.

They mounted to the skies,
And read deep mysteries;
While yet on earth, they placed a ladder there,
Like Jacob's, that each round should lead,
By prayer outspoken, in a word or deed,
The soul to heights of clearer, purer air.

They saw no messenger of gloom
In him whom we call Death, nor met their doom
As prisoner his sentence: but naturally as bud
unfolds to flower,
As child to man, so man to angel—
They recognizing death the glad evangel,
Leading to higher scenes of life and power.

THE ELEVENTH HOUR.

FAINT and worn and aged
    One stands knocking at a gate,
Though no light shines in the casement,
    Knocking though so late.
It has struck eleven
In the courts of heaven,
    Yet he still doth knock and wait.

While no answer cometh
    From the heavenly hill,
Blessed angels wonder
    At his earnest will.
Hope and fear but quicken
While the shadows thicken;
    He is knocking, knocking still.

Grim the gate unopened
    Stands with bar and lock:
Yet within the unseen Porter
    Hearkens to the knock.
Doing and undoing,
Faint and yet pursuing,
    This man's feet are on the Rock.

With a cry unceasing,
   Knocketh, prayeth he:
"Lord, have mercy on me
   When I cry to Thee."
With a knock unceasing,
And a cry increasing:
   "O my Lord! remember me."

Still the Porter standeth,
   Love-constrained He standeth near,
While the cry increaseth
   Of that love and fear:
"Jesus, look upon me—
Christ, hast Thou foregone me?—
   If I must, I perish here."

Faint the knocking ceases,
   Faint the cry and call:
Is he lost indeed forever,
   Shut without the wall?
Mighty Arms surround him,
Arms that sought and found him,
   Held, withheld, and bore through all.

Oh, celestial mansion!
   Open wide the door:

Crown and robes of whiteness,
Stone inscribed before,
Flocking angels bear them;
Stretch thy hand and wear them;
Sit thou down for evermore.

"BRINGING OUR SHEAVES WITH US."

THE time for toil is past, and night has come,
   The last and saddest of the harvest eves;
Worn out with labor long and wearisome,
Drooping and faint, the reapers hasten home,
   Each laden with his sheaves.

Last of the laborers, Thy feet I gain,
   Lord of the harvest! and my spirit grieves
That I am burdened, not so much with grain
As with a heaviness of heart and brain.
   Master, behold my sheaves!

Few, light, and worthless—yet their trifling weight
   Through all my frame a weary aching leaves;
For long I struggled with my hapless fate,
And staid and toiled till it was dark and late—
   Yet these are all my sheaves!

"BRINGING OUR SHEAVES WITH US."

Full well I know I have more tares than wheat—
  Brambles and flowers, dry stalks, and withered
    leaves;
Wherefore I blush and weep, as at Thy feet
I kneel down reverently, and repeat,
  "Master, behold my sheaves!"

I know these blossoms, clustering heavily
  With evening dew upon their folded leaves,
Can claim no value nor utility—
Therefore shall fragrancy and beauty be
  The glory of my sheaves.

So do I gather strength and hope anew;
  For well I know thy patient love perceives
Not what I did, but what I strove to do—
And though the full, ripe ears be sadly few,
  Thou wilt accept my sheaves.

THE MEETING PLACE.

I.

THE daylight has faded over the sea,
   The shadows are gathering heavily,
   The waters are moaning drearily,
And there is no haven in sight for me—
   Only a black, wild, angry haven ;
   Only a rolling, moaning sea ;
   And a small, weak bark by the tempest driven
Hither and thither helplessly.
   For I am alone on this moaning sea ;
   Alone, alone, on the wide, wild sea !
   Only God stands by in the dark by me,
But His silence is worse to bear than the moan
   Of the dreary waters that will not stay ;
And I am alone—ay, worse than alone,
   For God stands by, and has nothing to say !
   And Death is creeping over to me—
   Creeping across the drear black sea—
   Creeping into the boat with me !
And he will sink the small, weak bark,
And I shall float out in the dreary dark,
   Dead, dead, on the wide, wild sea ;
   A dead face up to the cruel sky—

Dead eyes that had wearied sore for the light—
A dead hand floating helplessly,
Tired with hard rowing through all the night;
This is what Thou shalt see, O God!
From Thy warm, bright home beyond the cloud
Thou denied'st me light, though it overflowed,
And there was not room for it all in heaven—
Thou denied'st one ray unto me, O God!
By the windy storm and tempest driven;
Thou shalt look on my lost face, God, and see
What it was to die in the dark for me!
But I can not reach Him with this wild cry—
I can not reach Him with this poor hand;
Peaceful He dwells in the peaceful land,
And the smile on His face is untouched by me—
Only another Eternity lost,
Only another poor soul gone down,
Far out at sea while He smileth on!
The songs of Heaven are loud and sweet,
And thrill His heart with joy; it is meet
That He should not catch the far-off moan
Of another soul undone—undone!
Here we part, O God!
Thou to Thy life and light,
To the home where Thy dear ones gather to Thee,
I to my Death and Night,
A lost thing, with nothing to do with Thee;

Drifting drearily out to sea.
Thou hast shut from Thee my feeble prayer;
  Let us part, O God!

II.

Through the darkness over the sea
A voice came calling—calling to me—
A gentle voice through the angry night,
And I thought, "Some one else is out to-night,
  Out, out, on the wide, wild sea;
  Can it be any one seeking me?"
So I answered as well as I could from my place,
Though the wind and rain were beating my face,
  And through the darkness, over the sea,
  Still the voice came calling, calling to me;
Nearer and nearer it came to me,
And one came into the boat from the sea.
The wind fell low round my little bark
As a wounded hand touched mine in the dark,
  And a weary head on my breast was laid;
And a trembling voice, as of one whom pain
  Had done to death, in a whisper said,
  "I had nowhere else to lay my head."

III.

And it was thus that He came to me:
I had spoken against Him bitterly,

As of one who sat smiling on in heaven—
  Smiling and resting peacefully—
While I was perishing tempest-driven;
  But it was thus that He came to me,
Through the deep waters struggling on,
Wherein standing or foothold found He none:
The wild wind beating about His face,
Fainting and sinking in that dark place;
He had been weary and far from home,
Struggling, forsaken, alone—alone!

So out in the night on the wide, wild sea,
  When the wind was beating drearily,
  And the waters were moaning wearily,
I met with Him who had died for me.

COME!

OH, word, of words the sweetest
    Oh, word, in which there lie
All promise, all fulfillment,
    And end of mystery!
Sorrowing or rejoicing,
    With doubt or terror nigh,
I hear the "Come!" of Jesus,
    And to His cross I fly.

Sometimes so far I've wandered,
  So lost I seem to be,
That faintly, like an echo,
  I hear the "Come to Me."
"Where art Thou, O Beloved?"
  Bewildered, sad, I cry;
Then, following the sweet summons,
  Till at His feet I lie.

Oh, soul! why shouldst thou wander
  From such a loving Friend?
Cling closer—closer to Him,
  Stay with Him to the end.
Alas! I am so helpless,
  So very full of sin,
Forever I am wandering
  And coming back again.

Oh, each time draw me nearer,
  That soon the "Come!" may be
Naught but a gentle whisper
  To one close, close to Thee;
Then, over sea or mountain,
  Far from or near my home,
I'll take Thy hand and follow,
  At that sweet whispered "Come!"

INTO HIS HANDS.

LUTHER'S HYMN.

COMMIT thou all thy griefs
    And ways into His hands;
To His sure truth and tender love
    Who earth and heaven commands
Who points the clouds their course;
    When wind and seas obey,
He shall direct thy wandering feet,
    He shall prepare thy way.

Put then thy trust in God;
    In duty's path go on;
Fix on His word thy steadfast eye,
    So shall thy work be done,
No profit canst thou gain
    By self-consuming care;
To Him commend thy cause, His ear
    Attends the softest prayer.

Give to the winds thy fear,
    Hope, and be undismayed,
God hears thy sighs, and counts thy tears—
    God shall lift up thy head.

Through waves and clouds and storm,
  He gently cleaves the way ;
Wait, then, His time ; the darkest night
  Shall end in brightest day.

Still heavy is thy heart ?
  Still sinks thy spirit down ?
Cast off the weight, let fear depart,
  And every care be gone.
What though thou rulest not,
  Yet earth and heaven and hell
Proclaim God sitteth on the throne,
  And doeth all things well.

Leave to His sovereign sway
  To choose and to command ;
So shalt thou, wondering, own His way
  How wise, how strong His hand ;
Far, far above thy thoughts
  His counsel shall appear
When fitly he the work hath wrought
  That caused thy needless fear.

Thou seest our weakness, Lord !
  Our hearts are known to Thee ;
Oh, lift then up the sinking heart,
  Confirm the feeble knee !

Let us in life, in death,
　Thy steadfast truth declare,
And publish with our latest breath
　Thy love and guardian care.

"MORTALLY WOUNDED."

I LAY me down to sleep,
　With little thought or care
Whether my waking find
　Me here — or *there!*

A bowing, burdened head,
　Only too glad to rest,
Unquestioning, upon
　A loving breast.

My good right hand forgets
　Her cunning now;
To march the weary march
　I know not how.

I am not eager, bold,
　Nor strong—all that is past!
I am willing *not to do*,
　At last, at last!

My half-day's work is done,
  And this is all my part :
I give a patient God
  My patient heart ;

And grasp His banner still,
  Though all its blue be dim ;
These stripes, no less than stars,
  Lead after Him.

Weak, weary and uncrowned,
  I yet *to bear* am strong ;
Content not even to cry,
  "How long ! How long !"

WITH FAITH AND PRAYER.

WITH faith and prayer,
    Dear Lord ! the burden Thou has sent
  I gladly bear,
For His dear sake who went—
With mortal anguish rent,
    Up Pilate's stair—
And from his judgment-hall
Bearing His cross in weakness for us all.

The faith, how small,
O Lord! with which I tread the way;
Give, at my call,
Faith that, from day to day,
Is fed by Christ alway.
I shall not fall;
But prove the promise blest,
"We which believe, *do* enter into rest."

The prayer, how weak,
O Lord! that lifts my heart to Thee.
But this I seek—
This one thing give to me—
Help my infirmity;
Within me speak,
And by the Spirit taught
I shall know what to pray for as I ought.

From pain and care,
O Lord! I seek not to be free.
But this my prayer—
Open my eyes to see
That Thou art leading me,
Then I can bear
To walk in darkness still,
Walking with Thee, submissive to Thy will.

Clouds come and go,
But, Lord, clouds only make more bright
　　The after glow !
After the darkest night
Will come the morning light,
　　And well I know
The morn itself may hide
Its face, but light shall be at even-tide.

Home is more near,
O Lord, by every passing day;
　　Home is more dear
By every prayer I pray—
By every footstep of the way
　　That brings me there.
Where Thou art, let me be,
For where Thou art is Home and Heaven to me.

"A little while!"
Dear Lord, the precious words are Thine!
　　A little while !
The blessed hope is mine,
Till on these eyes shall shine
　　Thy radiant smile,
And Thine own hand of grace
Shall wipe all tears from my uplifted face.

"THIS I DID FOR THEE—WHAT DOEST THOU FOR ME?"

I GAVE my life for thee,
  My precious blood I shed,
That thou might'st ransomed be,
  And quickened from the dead.
I gave my life for thee;
What hast thou given for me?

I spent long years for thee
  In weariness and woe,
That one eternity
  Of joy thou might'st know;
I spent long years for thee;
Hast thou spent one for me?

My Father's house of light,
  My rainbow-circled throne,
I left for earthly night,
  For wanderings sad and lone;
I left it all for thee;
Hast thou left aught for me?

I suffered much for thee,
  More than thy tongue can tell,

Of bitterest agony,
  To rescue thee from hell;
I suffered much for thee;
  What dost thou bear for me?

And I have brought to thee,
  Down from my home above,
Salvation full and free,
  My pardon and my love;
Great gifts I brought to thee;
  What hast thou brought to me?

O let thy life be given,
  Thy years for me be spent,
World-fetters all be riven,
  And joy with suffering blent;
Give thou thyself to me,
  And I will welcome thee!

—*Motto placed under a print of Christ in the study of a German divine.*

HE IS MY SHEPHERD.

HE is my Shepherd, I His sheep;
    I do not want to know
Whether the way be soft or steep
    By which I am to go,

If green and smooth the mountains be,
  I need not ask for more;
If stony, He will carry me,
  As He has done before.

He is my Shepherd, I His sheep;
  We travel onward still,
By pools, where water-lilies sleep,
  By many a quiet hill;
I feed in many a grassy dell,
  I drink the waters clear;
The gracious Voice I know so well,
  Is music to my ear.

He is my Shepherd, I His sheep;
  I wandered once, I know;
I heard Him on the mountains weep,
  That I should leave Him so.
I trembled, as I faintly guessed
  A sorrow so divine,
For as He clasped me to His breast
  The blood gushed forth on mine.

He is my Shepherd, I His sheep,
  And what if death be near?
The shadows up the valley creep,
  And yet I do not fear;

As closer to His side I cling,
   I feel the way so true
With which His love was pledged to bring
   And safe has brought me through.

He is my Shepherd, I His sheep;
   We journey on and on,
At last a smile upon His lips
   Shall tell me all is won.
The table that He spreads for me
   My foes shall all behold,
And in these trembling fingers see
   His cup of royal gold.

The cup He put so gently by,
   When death was drawing near,
He freely fills for such as I,
   And tells me not to fear.
And for those funeral odors shed
   Upon His dying brow,
He pours the oil of joy instead
   On each disciple now.

Shepherd! Good Shepherd! turn and see
   I follow far behind,
Thy voice of mercy calling me,
   Comes borne on every wind.

Set wide Thy Father's open door,
That I the light may see,
And in His house forevermore
At last abide with Thee.

WALKING IN WHITE.

O LORD my God, 'tis early dawn,
   And I would walk with Thee to-day!
Clothe me in garments white and clean,
All bright and beautiful, I pray.
Grant I may walk with greatest care,
So I may keep their lustre bright;
To-day, my Father, hear my prayer,
And let me walk with Thee in white.

The road was thorny yesterday,
Because I walked so far from Thee;
Yet oft I heard Thee kindly say,
"Come nearer, child; come near to
With garments soiled on yester-eve,
I grieved to view the painful sight;
To-day, my Father, O reprieve,
And let me walk with Thee in white!

Now may I plunge within the tide—
That fount for all our grief and woe,
Once opened in my Saviour's side;
'Twill make my garments white as snow,
With hands and feet, with head and heart,
All clean and pure before Thy sight.
Not for one moment, Lord, depart,
But let me walk with Thee in white!

No thought, no word, no deed to-day,
Which may displease my blessed Lord;
No idle loitering by the way,
But sweetly trusting in Thy Word.
Whate'er my hands may find to do,
That may I do with all my might:
To-day, my Father, pure and true,
Grant I may walk with Thee in white.

The failures of the yesterday,
The cares which may to-morrow come;
Each tear, each fear, now chase away,
And guide me on my journey home.
And when the evening shadows fall,
And I come kneeling in Thy sight,
Then may I feel, my Lord, my all,
That I have walked with Thee in white.

And can I walk each day with Thee,
With robes all white, and pure and clean?
Oh, tell me, Saviour, can I flee,
Forever from that monster—sin?
I know that in our home above,
Thy saints in all their full delight
Shall bask within redeeming love,
And always walk with Thee in white.

THE CROSS-BEARER.

WHEN I set out to follow Jesus,
    My Lord a cross held out to me;
Which I must take, and bear it onward,
    If I would His disciple be.
    I turned my head another way.
    And said, Not this, my Lord, I pray!

Yet, as I could not quite refuse Him,
    I sought out many another kind,
And tried among those painted crosses
    The smallest of them all to find.
    But still the Lord held forth my own
    This must thou bear, and this alone.

Unheeding then my dear Lord's offer,
  My burdens all on Him to lay,
I tried myself my cross to lighten,
  By cutting part of it away.
    And still the more I tried to do,
    The rest of it more heavy grew.

Well, if I can not go without it,
  I'll make the most of it I may;
And so I held my cross uplifted,
  In sight of all who came that way.
    Alas! my pride found bitterly,
    My cross looked small to all but me!

And then I was ashamed to bear it,
  Where others walked so free and light,
And trailed it in the dust behind me,
  And tried to keep it out of sight.
    Till Jesus said, Art thou indeed
    Ashamed to follow as I lead?

No! no!—Why, this shall be my glory—
  All other things I'll count but loss;
And so I even fashioned garlands,
  And hung them round about my cross.
    Ah, foolish one! such works are dead:
    Bear it *for me*, the Master said.

And still I was not prompt to mind Him,
   But let my self-will choose the way;
And sought me out new forms of service,
   And would do all things but obey.
     My Lord! I bless Thee for the pain
     That drove my heart to Thee again.

I bore it then, with Him before me,
   Right onward through the day's white heat
Till, with the toil and pain o'ermastered,
   I fainting fell down at His feet.
     But for His matchless care that day,
     I should have perished where I lay.

But oh, I grew so very weary,
   When life and sense crept back once more
The whole horizon hung with darkness,
   And grief where joy had been before;
     Better to die, I said, and rest,
     Than live with such a burden pressed.

Then Jesus spoke: Bring here thy burden,
   And find in me a full release;
Bring all thy sorrows, all thy longings,
   And take instead my perfect peace.
     Trying to bear thy cross alone!—
     Child, the mistake is all thine own.

And now my cross is all supported,—
Part on my Lord, and part on me:
But as He is so much the stronger,
  He seems to bear it—I go free.
    I touch its weight, just here and here,—
    Weight that would crush, were He not near

Or if at times it seemeth heavy;
  And if I droop along the road;
The Master lays his own sweet promise*
  Between my shoulder and the load:
    Bidding my heart look up, not down,
    Till the cross fades before the crown.

FINISHED WORK.

FINISHED work! For Jesus dieth;
  Woes and stripes and sufferings cease.
Finished work! For Jesus liveth,
  Leaving us His perfect peace.

Finished work! Oh, blessed promise,
  Toiling, fainting by the way;
Finished work shall we accomplish
  If we only watch and pray.

* " The pillow of the promise."—*Rutherford.*

Finished work! Oh, Holy Spirit,
　　Help our faith and keep us pure!
Finished work! The Master saith it,
　　Like the rock His word is sure.

Finished work! When it is ended,
　　Perfect love shall cast out fear.
Finished work! Co-working with Him,
　　In His form shall we appear.

Finished work! Oh, glorious foretaste!
　　Leaning then on Jesus' breast;
Finished work! No tears, no sorrow,
　　But eternal, heavenly rest.

"*POST TENEBRAS LUX.*"

IT is His way, and so it must be right;
　　Although at every step some foot that bleeds
Leaves prints of anguish, still our Father leads
　　Through the darkness unto light.
So dark it seems! We long for break of day;
We know not Jesus on the midnight flood.
Ah, once He trod the path of woe and blood,
　　His solitary way!

And yet that path of deepest gloom and woe
Led up to glory, greater for the cross
To which He bowed in life-long want and loss,
   With " Father, even so ! "
For midnight darkness often bears within
Its baffling blackness germs of heaven's light;
God's holiness is not one ray less bright
   For all this dark world's sin.

He holds us in the hollow of His hand,
And gives us light as we can bear it now.
His glory's shadow upon Moses' brow
   Was brightness far too grand
For sinful Israel's eyes to look upon ;
Yet those whose patient hearts seek daily strength
Shall surely have the eagle's wings at length,
   To mount toward the sun.

And eagle's vision, clear and bright and
      strong,
E'en here is given those whose hearts are pure ;
They, seeing Him invisible, endure,
   Although the way be long.
To them a light ariseth ; and the day,
Hid from Egyptian eyes by dark eclipse,
Shines bright as noon, and on their trustful lip
   Wakes praises while they pray.

And so we need no longer vainly grope,
Moaning the poet's death-cry, "Light, more
   light!"
We need not earth's dark lanterns, for the night
   Is brilliant with the hope
Of fairer day-dawn than e'er blessed the hills
Of God around Jerusalem of old.
Aye! while we watch the east, a flush of gold
   The glad horizon fills.

For God is light itself; in Him we know
There is no darkness; and when we at last
Dwell in Him truly, darkness shall be past,
   And life be all aglow.
O Christian! as the bird that sings at night,
Or, as the bird that God has taught to wait
Until the daybreak, sing at heaven's gate,
   For, "after darkness, light!"

BEAUTIFUL HANDS.

SUCH beautiful, beautiful hands,
   They're neither white nor small,
And you, I know, would scarcely think
   That they were fair at all.

I've looked on hands whose form and hue
A sculptor's dream might be,
Yet are these aged wrinkled hands
Most beautiful to me.

Such beautiful, beautiful hands—
　Though heart was weary and sad,
These patient hands kept toiling on,
　That the children might be glad.
I almost weep, as looking back
　To childhood's distant day,
I think how these hands rested not
　When mine were at their play.

Such beautiful, beautiful hands,
　They're growing feeble now;
For time and pain have left their mark
　On hand and heart and brow.
Alas! alas! the nearing time,
　And the sad, sad day to me,
When 'neath the daisies, out of sight,
　These hands will folded be.

But oh, beyond this shadow-lamp,
　Where all is bright and fair,
I know full well these dear old hands
　Will palms of victory bear.

Where crystal streams, through endless years,
  Flow over golden sands,
And where the old grow young again,
  I'll clasp my mother's hands.

MY SHIPS.

I.

AH, years ago!—no matter where,
  Beneath what roof or sky,
I dreamed of days, perhaps remote,
When ships of mine that were afloat
  Should in the harbor lie,
And all the costly freights they bore
Enrich me both in mind and store.

What dreams there were of Argosies,
  Laden in many a clime;
So stoutly built, so bravely manned,
No fear but they would come to land
  At their appointed time;
And I should see them, one by one,
Close furl their sails in summer's sun.

And then, while men in wonder stood,
  My ships I would unlade;

My treasures vast they should behold,
And to my learning and my gold
  What honors would be paid!
And though the years might come and go,
I could but wiser, richer grow.

II.

In later years,—no matter where,
  Beneath what roof or sky,
I saw the dreams of days remote
Fade out, and ships that were afloat,
  As drifting wrecks go by,
And all the many freights they bore
Lay fathoms deep, or strewed the shore.

While ships of which I never thought
  Were sailing o'er the sea;
And one by one, with costlier lade,
In safety all the voyage made,
  And brought their freights to me;
What I had lost but trifle seemed,
And I was richer than I dreamed!

No wondering crowd, with envious eye,
  Looked on my treasures rare;
Yet they were weightier far than gold;
They still increase, though I grow old,

And are beyond compare :
Would all the restless hearts I see,
Had ships like those that came to me?

IN THE FIELD.

FIGHTING the Battle of Life!
    With a weary heart and head;
For in the midst of the strife
    The banners of joy are fled,
Fled and gone out of sight,
    When I thought they were so near,
And the music of hope this night
    Is dying away on my ear.

Fighting alone to-night—
    With not even a stander-by
To cheer me in the fight,
    Or to hear me when I cry.
Only the Lord can hear,
    Only the Lord can see
The struggle within, how dark and drear,
    Though quiet the outside be.

Lord, I would fain be still
    And quiet behind my shield!

But make me to love Thy will,
  For fear I should ever yield;
Even as now, my hands,
  So doth my folded will
Lie waiting Thy commands,
  Without one anxious thrill.

But, as with sudden pain,
  My hands unfold and clasp—
So doth my will start up again,
  And taketh its old arm grasp.
Nothing but perfect trust
  And love of Thy perfect will,
Can raise me out of the dust,
  And bid my fears be still.

O Lord, Thou hidest Thy face,
  And the battle clouds prevail;
O grant me Thy most sweet grace,
  That I may not utterly fail!
Fighting alone to-night!
  With what a sinking heart—
Lord Jesus, in the fight,
  O stand not Thou apart!

REVIVED.

BREAK out, my heart, in joyous strain,
The sun has conquered night's sad reign,
And sheds down radiance clear;
Soon as the King turned round his face,*
My sorrow gave to rapture place!
 Now light and life are here,
  The spices flow
  God's work to show,
 Within His garden wrought.
  O Lord, my Lord!
  By Thy dear Word,
How is my heart continually restored!

My soul in doubt and bondage lay,
And all my joy had fled away—
 I sought Him, He was gone!
My pardon I could call to mind,
But still my Lord I could not find—
 'Twas day without the sun!

---

*" While the King turns round, my spikenard sendeth forth th
smell thereof."—*German Bible*.
 In our version the words are:
   " Sitteth at his table."

REVIVED. 251

Then near He drew,
And touched me, too,
With His most gracious hand;
O Saviour mine,
That touch of Thine
A Fountain proves of balsam most divine.

Blessing, salvation, Life and Light,
And all my wealth, and all my might
  On look of Thine depend;
Just as when earth lies steeped in dew,
Let but the morning sun break through,
    Scents from wak'd flowers ascend;
      In my heart's ground,
      The blossoms found,
    Breathe sweet upturned to Thee!
      When Thy beams bright
      Dispel the night,
They raise their drooping faces to the light.

Hosannas to my sun I'll raise,
Break forth, my heart, in joy and praise,
    Break forth in happy song!
Lord, I am all too weak to sing,
I only stammer out, my King,
    Thanks that to Thee belong.

Wake up, my heart,
All fear, all smart,
Thy Saviour's touch can heal.
Lord Christ, to Thee
All glory be,
Who art the same throughout eternity!

GRANDFATHER'S PET.

THIS is the room where she slept,
    Only a year ago—
Quiet, and carefully swept,
    Blinds and curtains like snow.
There, by the bed in the dusty gloom,
    She would kneel with her tiny clasped hands and pray!
Here is the little white rose of a room,
    With the fragrance fled away!

Nelly, grandfather's pet,
    With her wise little face—
I seem to hear her yet
    Singing about the place;
But the crowds roll on, and the streets are drear,
    And the world seems hard with a bitter doom
And Nelly is singing elsewhere and here
    Is the little white rose of a room.

Why, if she stood just there,
    As she used to do,
With her long, light yellow hair,
    And her eyes of blue—
If she stood, I say, at the edge of the bed,
    And ran to my side with a living touch,
Though I know she is quiet and buried and dead
    I should not wonder much;

For she was so young, you know—
    Only seven years old,
And she loved me, loved me so,
    Though I was gray and old;
And her face was so wise, and so sweet to see,
    And it still looked living, when she lay dead,
As she used to plead for mother and me
    By the side of that very bed!

I wonder now, if she
    Knows I am standing here,
Feeling, wherever she be,
    We hold the place so dear?
It can not be that she sleeps too sound,
    Still in her little night-gown dressed,
Not to hear my footsteps sound
    In the room where she used to rest.

I have felt hard fortune's stings,
  And battled in doubt and strife,
  And never thought much of things
    Beyond this human life;
But I can not think that my darling died
  Like great, strong men, with their prayers un-
      true—
Nay, rather she sits at God's own side,
  And sings as she used to do!

TRUST.

I CAN NOT see, with my short human sight,
  Why God should lead this way or that for me.
I only know He saith, "Child, follow me;"
    But I can trust.

I know not why my path should be at times
So straightly hedged, so strangely barred before,
I only know God *could* keep wide the door;
    But I can trust.

I find no answer, often, when beset
With questions fierce and subtle on my way,
And often have but strength to faintly pray;
    But I can trust.

I often wonder, as with trembling hand
I cast the seed along the furrowed ground,
If ripened fruit for God will there be found;
    But I can trust.

I can not know why suddenly the storm
Should rage so fiercely round me in its wrath;
But this I know, God watches all my path;
    And I can trust.

I may not draw aside the mystic veil
That hides the unknown future from my sight,
Nor know if for me waits the dark or light;
    But I can trust.

I have no power to look across the tide,
To know, while here, the land beyond the river
But this I know, I shall be God's forever!
    So I can trust.

JERUSALEM THE GOLDEN.

JERUSALEM the Golden,
    I languish for one gleam
Of all thy glory folden
    In distance, and in dream!

My thoughts like palms in exile,
   Climb up to look and pray
For a glimpse of that dear country
   That lies so far away.

Jerusalem the Golden,
   Methinks each flower that blows
And every bird a-singing,
   Of the same secret knows!
I know not what the flowers
   Can feel, or singers see,
But all these summer raptures
   Are prophecies of thee.

Jerusalem the Golden,
   When sun-set 's in the west,
It seems the gate of glory,
   Thou city of the blest!
And midnight's starry torches,
   Through intermediate gloom,
Are waving with their welcome,
   To thy eternal home.

Jerusalem the Golden,
   Where loftily they sing,
O'er pain and sorrows olden,
   Forever triumphing!

Lowly may be thy portal
  And dark may be the door,
The mansion is immortal!—
  God's palace for His poor.

Jerusalem the Golden,
  There all our birds that flew,—
Our flowers but half unfolden,
  Our pearls that turn'd to dew,—
And all the glad life music
  Now heard no longer here,
Shall come again to greet us,
  As we are drawing near.

Jerusalem the Golden,
  I toil on day by day;
Heart-sore each night with longing,
  I stretch my hands and pray
That midst thy leaves of healing
  My soul may find her nest,
Where the wicked cease from troubling
  The weary are at rest.

AFTER THE BATTLE.

MY wound is deep, I fain would sleep, O Lord
   I stretch my hands to Thee!
Do Thou according to Thy faithful word,
   And set Thy servant free!

Sore hath the battle been, but Victory
   Crowned me as evening fell;
Now heart and flesh are failing, let me see
   The land where I would dwell.

The battle-field is cold and silent now,
   Its thunders sunk to rest;
And I can feel the touch upon my brow
   Of low winds from the West;

The clouds of sleep, the last and longest sleep,
   Are heavy on mine eyes;
They can not watch, dear Lord, they can not weep
   Beneath Thy dark'ning skies.

What time the angel, Victory, came down
   To bid my conflict cease,
And crowned my tired soul with the shining crown
   Of Righteousness and Peace,

That instant broke the sound as of a knell
  On the faint evening's breath;
And on my parched mouth, like the dew there fell
  The soft, sweet kiss of Death;

For Victory and Death walk hand in hand
  Down all the battle-field—
One ruddy as the dawn, the other grand,
  But pale behind his shield;

And whom God loves, to whom is victory
  On such a field as this,
Receive the radiant angel's crown, and see
  The pale cold angel's kiss;

That kiss has made my spirit faint and weak;
  Lord, take me to Thy breast;
Oh, fold me closely, where the weariest seek
  And find Eternal Rest!

Christ, who has been my perfect sun by day,
  Will be my star by night;
On my deep rest the Lord shall shine alway,
  An everlasting Light.

Dimly I see Him, through the clouds that roll
  Along the dark'ning West:
O Lord, my Star, by Thy sweet light my soul
  Doth enter into Rest.

THE CLOUD VISION.

IN the chill December weather,
    When the earth all barren lies;
When the dead leaves drift together
    And the feathery snow-flake flies;
When *thus* ends the Spring-time sowing,
    Summer's brightness, beauty, light,
Autumn, too, its fruits bestowing;
    Then how drear the grave's dark night!

Such the thought, when toward God's acre,
    'Mid broad fields and woodlands found,
We went forth in midst of winter,
    There to make in frozen ground,
And where all was bare and leafless,
    Resting place for baby's head;
Which so oft, when tired and restless,
    We had laid on downy bed.

Rough winds blew the falling snow-flakes;
    Clouds dropped low like funeral pall,
O'er the grave where we with heart-ache
    Asked, "Of life, can this be all?"—
And took up our baby darling,
    There to lay him, side by side,
With his sister, softly sleeping;
    Who, ere he was born, had died.

Scarcely was the sad rite ended,
  And our little one at rest;
When beneath the clouds, now lifted,
  Shone the sun from out the West;
Filling earth and sky with beauty;
  Painting clouds with gorgeous hue;
Opening up the path of glory;
  Bringing gates of pearl to view.

Slowly changed the sunset splendor,
  As the evening shades drew nigh,
Into light of clearest amber,
  All along the western sky;
When two clouds, of scarce a hand-breadth,
  Just above the sun were seen,
All aglow with light that answered
  To its beams of golden sheen.

There they stood, as might God's angels,
  Ling'ring on the heavenly heights,
When come back from glad evangels
  Taking note of their long flights:
Then, as if one thought possessing,
  Nearer to each other drew;
And, as though in fond caressing,
  Vanished quickly out of view.

Twas as though our baby children
    Stood transfigured to our sight :
One, come forth from gate of Heaven,
    And from out its mansions bright;
Welcome bringing to the other,
    Hast'ning from the earth away :—
Sister welcoming the brother
    To the realms of endless day.

Was it not a heavenly vision
    Which our Lord in pity sent?
Was not this its kindly mission—
    This His merciful intent,
Our grieved hearts to keep from murmur,
    O'er this second bitter cup :
Which that day in bleak December,
    To our lips we lifted up?

MERCY BEFORE SACRIFICE.

"Come unto me and I will give you rest."

COME to the clear deep river,
    Come where the pastures call;
Give to the great good Giver
    The trust that is thy all.

From want eternal fleeing,
   Come to an endless store;
Bring thy whole famished being,
   For He wants nothing more.

If thoughts of thine appall thee,
   Oh, lean on His and live!
To sacrifice they call thee,
   While He is here *to give*.
Accept thy Father's measure
   Of need that He can see.
The heart to do His pleasure
   Is in His love for thee.

He will not now refuse thee,
   Weak hand and vision dim :
For something He will use thee,
   But first thou wantest Him.
The spirit worn with straying,
   Will find His judgment best;
Oh, hear what He is saying,
   And yield thyself to rest.

For one transporting minute
   The beckoning word obey :
There is a power within it
   To bear thee on thy way.

That voice of mercy speaking
Is God the Saviour's might,
And all thy heart is seeking
Lies safely in its light.

"IT MIGHT HAVE BEEN."

LED by kindlier hand than ours,
    We journey through this earthly scene,
And should not, in our weary hours,
    Turn to regret what might have been.

And yet these hearts, when torn by pain,
    Or wrung by disappointment keen,
Will seek relief from present cares
    In thoughts of joys that might have been.

But let us still these wishes vain;
    We know not that of which we dream.
Our lives might have been sadder yet;
    God only knows what might have been.

Forgive us, Lord, our little faith;
    And help us all, from morn till e'en,
Still to believe that lot the best
    Which is--not that which might have been

And grant we may so pass the days
The cradle and the grave between,
That death's dark hour not darker be
For thoughts of what life might have been.

A VERY PRESENT HELP IN TROUBLE.

TRUST in the Lord! yea, trust in Him;
  Renew thy strength again;
For He, from whom thy faith was born,
  That faith will still sustain.

Commit thy way to Him, to whom
  Thou dost commit thy soul;
He sees the path by thee unseen:
  On Him thy burden roll.

Wait thou on Him; His time is best;
  His wisdom shall declare:
Wait thou in patient hope, and trace
  A Father's tender care.

Rest upon Him, on Him, thy Lord,
  Till thou canst see His face;
Folded within each purpose lie
  Deep mysteries of grace.

He nourishes the comfortless:
　　He sends thee gloomy days,
To train thy soul for nobler flight,
　　And give thee themes for praise.

He sends the blast; He bids the storm
　　Sweep o'er His richest land,
To prove the trees of righteousness
　　Are planted by His hand.

He lets the tear-mist float above
　　The valley's fairest spot;
And the budding grass is greenest where
　　Our earthly joys are not.

He sends His springs among the hills,
　　When other streams decline;
And where the flowery gourd hath drooped,
　　He trains His fruitful vine.

Whoso is wise, and all His works
　　With watchful care discern,
The loving-kindness of the Lord
　　They, even they, shall learn.

A LITTLE WHILE.

A LITTLE while of mingled joy and sorrow,
    A few more years to wander thus below;
To wait the dawning of that golden morrow,
    When morn shall break above our night of woe.

A few more thorns about our pathway growing,
    Ere yet our hands may cull the heavenly flowers;
The morning comes, but, first, the tearful sowing,
    Ere we repose these weary souls of ours.

A few more hours of weariness and sighing,
    Of mourning o'er the power of inner sin;
A little while of daily crucifying,
    To this vain world, the evil heart within.

A little longer in this vale of weeping,
    Of yearning for the sinless home above:
A little while our marriage garments keeping
    Unspotted, by the power of Him we love.

A little while for winning souls to Jesus,
    Ere we behold His beauty face to face;
A little while for healing soul diseases,
    By telling others of a Saviour's grace.

A little while to spread the joyful story
   Of Him who made our guilt and curse His own
A little while ere we behold the glory,
   To gain fresh jewels for our heavenly crown.

A little while, then we shall dwell forever
   Within our bright, our everlasting home,
Where time, or space, or death can no more sever
   Our grief-wrung hearts, and pain can never come.

'Tis but a *little* while; the way is dreary,
   The night is dark, but we are nearing land;
Oh, for the rest of heaven, for we are weary,
   And long to mingle with the deathless band!

MIGHTY TO SAVE.

Isaiah lxiii. 1.

THE King of Glory standeth
   Beside that heart of sin,
His mighty voice commandeth
   The raging waves within.
The floods of deepest anguish
   Roll backward at His will,
As o'er the storm ariseth
   His mandate, "Peace be still."

At times with *sudden* glory,
  He speaks and all is done;
Without one stroke of battle
  The victory is won.
While we with joy beholding
  Can scarce believe it true,
That e'en our Kingly Jesus
  Can form such hearts anew.

He comes in blood-stained garments;
  Upon His brow a crown;
The gates of brass fly open,
  The iron bands drop down.
From off the fettered captive
  The chains of Satan fall,
While angels shout triumphant
  That Christ is Lord of all.

But sometimes in the stillness
  He gently draweth near,
And whispers words of welcome
  Into the sinner's ear;
With anxious heart awaiteth
  The answer to His cry,
The oft-repeated question,
  Oh, wherefore wilt thou die?

Or in the gathering darkness,
   With wounded feet and sore,
The suppliant Saviour standeth,
   And knocketh at the door.
The bleak winds howl around Him;
   The unbelief and sin;
Yet Jesus waits, entreating
   That He may enter in.

He whispers through the portal,
   He woos us with His love;
He calls us to the kingdom
   That waits for us above.
He speaks of all the gladness
   His yearning heart would give
Tells of the flowing fountain,
   And bids us wash and live.

O Christ, Thy love is mighty!
   Long-suffering is Thy grace!
And glorious is the splendor
   That beameth from Thy face!
Our hearts upleap in gladness
   When we behold that love;
As we go singing onward,
   To dwell with Thee above!

"TENEO ET TENEOR."

"I HOLD and I am held!" What hold I to,
And what holds me? I hold Thy cross,
thou Word
Of the Eternal! Where the envious Jew
Pierced Thee, my fingers press, nor can be
stirred,
Though hell oppose! By Thee my soul is held!
By all Gethsemane's agony and grief
United, joined, and naught can break the weld
But my own want of faith—my unbelief!

O God of Calvary: O Lord divine!
Hold me and I am held! I can not slide
When pressing closely to Thy bleeding side,
Though men and devils 'gainst my soul combine'
Nor shall I wander far, if in the veil
Of Jesus' flesh, my anchor has been cast ;
But I shall hear the welcome plaudit—" Hail,
Beloved, enter into rest!" at last.

BETHANY.

SIX days before the Passover
   The blessed Saviour came
To Bethany, where He remained
   Until His hour of shame;
His last abode was in the home
   Of Lazarus, His friend:
Those He had loved while in the world
   He loved unto the end.

The shadow of the Passion lay
   Brooding on all around,
Though what it meant they could not know
   Its depth was too profound
For mortal eye to search it out—
   Though woman's * love might see
Further than most into the shade
   Of that great Mystery.

His sacred Heart in its lone depths
   Was heaving at the thought
That human nature's perfectness
   Through suffering must be wrought.

* St. Matt. xxvi. 12.

And yet He set His face to go
  With firm endurance on,
And rose above the nature weak
  That clothed the Eternal Son:

And He did then for evermore
  That form of trial bless,
If only sinking hearts to Him
  Will turn in their distress;
One ray of glory in the Crown
  That on His brows is set,
Is drawn from those deep pangs of **Fear**
  He never can forget.

Not for Himself alone He fears—
  That all-foreseeing Eye
Distinguishes each single throb
  Of human agony;
He wept o'er every closing grave,
  Unto the end of time;
His soul drank in the rising swell
  Of sorrow's awful chime.

He took full measure of the grief
  Of every separate saint,
As one by one, each on his cross
  Must tremble and grow faint;

He knew, though He had given them rest,
    They first must find sore strife,
Must seek e'en through the gates of Death
    His promised gift of Life.

Yet even then His joy arose
    Forever to increase,
In knowing that this suffering host
    Would find in Him their peace;
The travail of His soul might bow
    That sacred Head to earth,
Yet He is satisfied to see
    The new Creation's birth.

He feels the presence of meek love
    Already at His side,
The gentle ones who cling to Him,
    And breast the world's strong tide;
He sees the eyes that to Him turn,
    The hands that seek His own,
Those who, in sharpest discipline,
    Trust Him, and Him alone.

Apostles, Martyrs, the long line
    Of royal, warrior soul,
Flash on Him their triumphant smiles
    From where the Future rolls;

The white-robed multitude, whom none
   Can number or declare,
Waft Him their floating voice of praise
   Already on the air.

Lord! since our griefs on Thee were laid,
   And Thou hast felt their sting,
Help us in holiest calm to take
   Our turn of suffering :
Thou didst look on unto Thy Joy,
   And so by grace will we,
But we would clasp Thy Cross, and feel
   We owe that Joy to Thee.

WAITING.

LORD of my nights and days !
   Let my desire be,
Not to be rid of earth,
   But nearer Thee—

If I may nearer draw
   Thro' lengthened grief and pain ;
Then to continue here,
   Must be my gain ;

Till I have strengthened been,
   To take a wider grasp

Of that Eternal Life
　I long to clasp;

Till I am so refined
　I can the glory bear,
Of that excess of joy
　I thirst to share;

Till I am meet to gaze
　On uncreated Light,
Transformed, and perfected,
　By that new sight.

Sorrow's long lesson o'er,
　Death's discipline gone through,
Thou wilt unfold to me
　What Joy can do.

Glad souls are on the wing,
　From Earth to Heaven they flee:
At last! Thine hour will come,
　To send for me.

Reveal the Mighty Love
　That binds Thy Heart to mine:
Thy Counsels and my will
　Should intertwine.

Lord of my heart and hopes !
  Let my desire be,
Not to be rid of Earth,
  But one with Thee.

ALPHA AND OMEGA.

ALPHA and Omega !
  Be Thou my First and Last !
The Source whence I descend,
The Joy to which I tend,
  When Earth is past.

Open my waking eyes,
  And fill them with Thy Light.
For Thee each plan begun,
In Thee each duty done,
  Close them at night.

Enfold me when asleep,
  Let soft dews from above
Refresh the long day's toil ;
Wash off the worldly soil,
  And strengthen Love.

Men speak of Four Last Things
Death, and the Judgment Hall,

Hell, and the Heaven so fair:
But Thou, O Lord! art there,
  Beyond them all.

There is no "last" with Thee,
  But only our last Sins,
Last Sorrows, and last Tears,
Last Sicknesses, last Fears,
  Then Joy begins:

Joy without bound or end,
  Concentric circles bright,
Spreading from round Thy Throne,
Flowing from Thee alone,
  O Love! O Light!

Lay Thy right Hand of Power
  In blessing on my brow;
Heaven's Keys are in Thy Hand,
Its Portals open stand:
  I fear not now.

Lead Thou me gently in,
  Thou who through Death hast past;
Then bring me to Thy Throne,
For Thee I seek alone,
  My First and Last.

INDEX TO SUBJECTS.

All is Known to Thee.	20
A Little While.	45
Alone, yet not Alone.	51
Anchor within the Veil, The	109
All is Light	123
Asleep on Guard	132
All in Christ	163
Abide with Us	170
After the Battle	258
A Little While	267
Alpha and Omega	277
A Very Present Help in Trouble	265
Border Lands, The	18
Bridegroom's Dove, The	35
Bridges	126
Burial of Moses, The	138
Better Life, The	172
Bringing our Sheaves with Us	219
Beautiful Hands	244
Bethany	272
Changed Cross, The	5
Call, The	82
Cross and Crown, The	86
Coming	116
Christian and his Echo, The	144
Comfort by the Way	141

INDEX TO SUBJECTS.

Christmas Hymn, A................................. 153
Communion with God 158
Cross, The.. 185
Crown, The 186
Come !... 224
Cross-Bearer, The................................. 238
Cloud Vision, The................................ 260

Delectable Mountains, The 107
Distractions in Prayer............................ 113
Drawing Water 175

Evening Prayer.................................... 62
Even Me 87
Eleventh Hour, The............................... 217
Euthanasy.. 215

Faith's Repose 106
Father, take my Hand 128
For the New Year 198
Footsteps on the Other Side...................... 210
Funeral Hymn..................................... 212
Finished Work 241

Gone Home 211
God our Strength................................. 15
God, my Exceeding Joy............................ 38
God's Support and Guidance....................... 41
God's Anvil...................................... 85
Grief was sent for thy Good...................... 96
God's Ways....................................... 111
Gracious Answer, The............................. 130
Grandfather's Pet................................ 252

Holy Tears 18

INDEX TO SUBJECTS. 281

Hinder me Not	47
Heaven	58
Hour of Prayer, The	134
Hymn of Trust	137
Himself hath Done it	165
He is my Shepherd	233

I Am	43
I Cling to Thee	50
In Heaven	72
It is I: Be not Afraid	75
It is well	183
Into His Hands	226
In the Field	248
"It Might Have Been"	264

Jerusalem the Golden	255

Lost Treasures	25
Leave Me not Now	105
Longings	124
Light and Darkness	157
Living Waters	167
Long Good-Night, The	208
Less and More	146

Meeting Place, The	9
My Times are in Thy Hands	16
Mary's Choice	32
My Lambs	78
My Guest	114
Ministry	181
Memories	191
Meeting Place, The	221
"Mortally Wounded"	228

My Ships	246
Mercy before Sacrifice	262
Mighty to Save	268
"Nearer Home"	33
Near Jesus	66
Nature and Faith	76
Now	141
Need of Jesus, The	142
Oh! for the Happy Days Gone By	22
One by One	31
Oh! to be Ready	34
Oh! my Saviour Crucified	89
Onward	95
O Lord! Thou knowest	179
Pilgrim, The	11
Pilgrim's Wants, The	56
Pilgrim of Earth	69
Peace of God, The	89
Peace	91
Prayer for Strength	93
Pray for Whom Thou Lovest	174
Perpetuity of Joy in Heaven	200
Pathways of the Holy Land	196
Prayer out of the Depths	187
"Post Tenebras Lux"	242
Quiet Mind, A	121
Return thee to thy Rest	65
Retrospect	148
Revived	250

INDEX TO SUBJECTS.

Sunday.. 27
School of Suffering................................... 52
Supplication.. 61
Scenes on Jordan's Strand............................ 97
Sufferer Cheered, The................................ 161
Salome 190

There is Light Beyond................................ 99
Thy Will be Done..................................... 135
Thy Will be Done..................................... 102
They Shall be Mine................................... 103
Tempest-Tossed, The.................................. 146
Time for Prayer, The................................. 156
True Dream, A.. 177
Through the Flood on Foot............................ 202
" This I Did for Thee—What doest Thou for Me?"...... 232
Trust.. 254
" Teneo et Teneor "................................. 271

Voice from Heaven, A................................. 59
Verdict of Death, The................................ 150

Wandering Heart, The 63
Wholly Resigned 15
Who is my Brother?................................... 68
What is this that He Saith?.......................... 71
Widow of Nain, The 194
Way, the Truth, and the Life, The.................... 154
We are the Lord's.................................... 214
With Faith and Prayer................................ 229
Walking in White..................................... 236
Waiting.. 275

INDEX TO FIRST LINES.

After long days of storms and showers.................................. 27
Alas! for the wildly wandering heart.............. 63
Amid the shadows and the fears 109
All in weakness, all in sorrow................................... 187
Another year, another year 198
Ah, years ago!—no matter where.................. A. D. F. R. 246
A little while of mingled joy and sorrow..................... 267
Alpha and Omega!...... 277

Beyond the smiling and the weeping. ....HORATIUS BONAR. 45
Beyond the stars that shine in golden glory........A. SHIPTON. 99
By Nebo's lonely mountain. .... MRS. C. F. ALEXANDER. 138
Breezes of spring, all earth to life awaking.......... 157
Break out, my heart, in joyous strain................ 250

Christ leads us through no darker rooms........RICH. BAXTER. 15
Come forth! come on with solemn song.............. 212
Commit thou all thy griefs...................... 226
Come to the clear, deep river................... A. L. WARING. 262

Early my spirit turned .. ..JAS. W. ALEXANDER. 39

Father, I know that all my life............... ANNA L. WARING. 16
Father, into Thy loving hands................... 18
Forsake me not, my God.. .... *Trans.* JAS. W. ALEXANDER. 41
Father of mercy! at the close of day. ....R. N. 62
Father! before Thy footstool kneeling. 93
Four little words, no more.... 101

(284)

INDEX TO FIRST LINES.

Father, beneath Thy sheltering wing..... 106
Faint, and worn, and aged. .. 217
Finished work! For Jesus dieth...... F. A. L. 241
Fighting the Battle of Life........ 248

Gone home! gone home! She lingers here no longer........ 211

Hinder me not! the path is long and weary........ 47
How few who from their youthful day 111
How doth Death speak of our beloved........ MRS. CHARLES. 150
Himself hath done it all........ 165
Here brief is the sighing........ 200
He is my Shepherd, I His sheep........ 233

It was a time of sadness. .. .. HON. MRS. CHARLES HOBART. 5
I want that adorning divine........ 56
I shine in the light of God... 59
I want to live near Jesus 66
I loved them so 78
I see them far away.. 107
I can not pray; yet, Lord, Thou knowest.... FRED. W. FABER. 113
I have a wonderful Guest....... 114
It may be in the evening........ MRS. B. MACANDREW. 116
I have a treasure which I prize... 121
I have a bridge within my heart........ A. D. F. R. 126
I need Thee, precious Jesus 142
I journey through a desert drear and wild. 147
In human form enthroned. 153
In Thee, my heart, O Jesus! finds repose........ 163
In some wild Eastern legend the story has been told.. 167
I had drank with lips unsated 175
I dreamt we danced in careless glee. 177
I journey forth rejoicing........ 208
I lay me down to sleep. 228
I gave my life for thee........ 232

I can not see with my short human sight............ 254
It is His way, and so it must be right....................... 242
In the chill December weather................ELDRIDGE MIX. 260
" I hold and I am held!" What hold I to?.......S. T. CLARK. 271

Jesus, engrave it on my heart...................... 32
Jerusalem the Golden........ 255

Let us be patient, God has taken from us 25
Lord, hear my prayer...... ....R. N. 61
Lord, I hear of showers of blessing... 87
Life's mystery—deep, restless as the ocean.... 91
Leave me not now while still the shade is creeping............ 105
Lord, I am come along with Thee 158
Lord of my nights and days!........ 275
Led by kindlier hands than ours ... . G. ZABRISKIE GRAY. 264

Man, in his weakness, needs a stronger stay.............. ... 15
My God, whose gracious pity I may claim ....S. R. M. 20
My Dove! The Bridegroom speaks 35
Must I my brother keep 68
Must Jesus bear the cross alone........... 86
My God, is any hour so sweet... 134
My wound is deep, I fain would sleep; O Lord........... ...
                                          B. MACANDREW. 258

Oh! for the happy days gone by............FRED. W. FABER. 22
One by one the sands are flowing............................. 31
One sweetly solemn thought ... .PHŒBE CARY. 33
Oh! to be ready when death shall come.................... 34
O holy Saviour! Friend unseen 50
Oh! heaven is nearer than mortals think..... 58
O Loving One! O Bounteous One!...................... 148
Oh! for the peace which floweth as a river.................... 71
O my Saviour crucified. 89

Oh, shame ! we're sometimes fain to say.. 132
Oh, Love Divine ! that stooped to share...... 137
Oh, word of words, the sweetest !........... MARY A. RANKIN. 224
O Lord, my God, 'tis early dawn ....S. J. CURRIER. 236

Pilgrim of earth, who art journeying to heaven.... 63
Pain's furnace-heat within me quivers...................... 85

Return, return thee to thy only rest... 65
Rise ! for the day is passing 141

Still onward through this land of foes......................... 11
Saviour, beneath Thy yoke 52
Silence filled the courts of heaven 72
Some there are who seem exempted............. 96
Say ! shall I take the thorn away ?........................... 161
Since service is the highest lot.............................. 181
So they said who saw the wonders........... 183
She knew not what for them she sought........MRS. CHARLES. 190
Sitting in my humble doorway......... 210
Such beautiful, beautiful hands........ ...ELLEN H. M. GATES. 244
Six days before the Passover. 272

Thou bidd'st us call 43
Tossed with rough winds and faint with fear............. 75
The night was dark ; behold, the shade was deeper.......... 82
Traveler, faint not on the road 95
There came a little child with sunny hair.......... 97
They shall be mine.. 103
The way is dark, my Father.... .... HENRY N. COBB. 128
The way is dark, my child.................. .. HENRY N. COBB. 130
True faith, producing love to God and man................... 144
Two Prayers, dear Lord, in One.... .... A. D. F. R. 146
Thou art the way .... MRS. CHARLES. 154
The tender light is fading where.............. H. N. POWERS. 170

INDEX TO FIRST LINES.

Thou knowest, Lord, the weariness and sorrow.... 179
The strongest light casts deepest shade.........MRS. CHARLES. 185
Thou shalt be crowned, O mother blest !. .....MRS. CHARLES. 186
Thy miracles are no state splendors...... .....MRS. CHARLES. 194
The pathways of Thy land are little changed...MRS. CHARLES. 196
The sun had sunk in the west.... . .....MRS. B. MACANDREW. 202
The time for toil is past..... 219
The daylight has faded over the sea......MRS. B. MACANDREW. 221
This is the room where she slept................. 252
The King of Glory standeth......... 268
Trust in the Lord ! yea, trust in Him...................... 265

We are the Lord's. His, earthly life and spirit.............. 214
We need no change of sphere............. 215
Where the faded flower shall freshen. ....HORATIUS BONAR. 9
When no kind earthly friend is near 51
We wept—'twas Nature wept, but Faith..................... 76
We ask for peace, O Lord ! 89
What though storm-clouds gather round me..... 123
When shall I be at rest ?..... 124
We see not, know not, all our way.. · ... JOHN G. WHITTIER. 135
When is the time for prayer ?..................... 156
When we reach a quiet dwelling................ 172
When fall the evening shadows long and deep......... ... 191
With faith and prayer.......... ....HENY N. COBB. 229
When I set out to follow Jesus................ANNA WARNER. 236

Yes, thou may'st weep.... 13
Yes, pray for whom thou lovest............................. 174

www.ingramcontent.com/pod-product-compliance
Lightning Source LLC
Chambersburg PA
CBHW032105220426
43664CB00008B/1138